PRAISE FOR MARK GORDON SMITH'S

Tuscan Echoes

". . . a dedicated quest to perceive and understand what is the essence of Italian life and culture. *Tuscan Echoes* is a superb and original extended meditation on nationality and identity." —MIDWEST BOOK REVIEW

". . . an exceptional travel book. . . . Author Mark G. Smith writes with such intimacy and intensely personal imagery that the reader can only imagine he/she is traveling side by side with the author." —ALLBOOKS REVIEW

"Readers who pick up this book should look for a calm widening of the spirit; there are no car chases, no wild sex, and no dives into the depths of human depravity. *Tuscan Echoes* is an examination of the ordinary in the world, an examination which, paradoxically, leads us to the discovery of the extraordinary." —SMOKY MOUNTAIN NEWS

"Exquisite travelogue memoir notable for its richly descriptive passages about place and its tenderness of spirit . . . a perfect love song to Italy." —CHARLESTON POST AND COURIER

"*Tuscan Echoes* is a strikingly intimate portal into Italy. Readers will appreciate it for its unique approach and sensual descriptions." —ITALIAN TRIBUNE

"At night, I pour myself a glass of Chianti, sit in my favorite chair, and for one sacred hour, I travel to the most beautiful country in the world—Italy. This book transcends genre; it's not only a marvelous travelogue but a unique history book that defines the heart of Italy as it seduces the reader into places filled with mystery and romance." —JACQUELINE DeGROOT

"This magical, marvelous, travel memoir captures the essence of Italian life. Mark's rich and textured style of writing invites the reader into the places he so accurately describes. I felt as if I was there. Truly a book everyone should read and have in their library if they are interested in, or love, Italy." —AMAZON.COM READER

Tuscan Light

Tuscan Light

Memories of Italy

MARK GORDON SMITH

Almar Books
Ocean Isle Beach, North Carolina

Tuscan Light: Memories of Italy copyright ©2007 by Mark Gordon Smith

Almar Books, Ocean Isle Beach, NC 28469 USA
www.almarbooks.com

First paperback edition, 2007

10 09 08 07   6 5 4 3 2 1
Printed in the United States

Library of Congress Control Number: 2007900313

ISBN-10: 0-9740983-4-5
ISBN-13: 978-0-9740983-4-0

Book and jacket design: October Publishing
Cover and interior photos: Mark Gordon Smith
Maps: Mark Gordon Smith

This book is dedicated to Gordon, Spray, Rob, and Judy Clack, with my deepest and unending gratitude.

Contents

Tables

Hands

Epilogue

Acknowledgments

In Italy, the people of Malmantile, the Guarnieri families, Anna and Luciano Mancini, Signora Bianca, and the workers who spend their years tending the grapes and the olives were the inspiration for this book. An inner light shines from them, hence the title of this work.

Alessandro Tombelli and Paolo Milazzo have shared hour upon hour with me as we traversed Italia. They have explained facets of Italian life that would never have been experienced otherwise. As you read this book, you will be introduced to all of the others who willingly took time to help me gain a more profound understanding of the Italian culture. My deepest appreciation is extended to them all.

Nicki Leone at October Publishing, Jacqueline DeGroot, and Barbara Brannon at Winoca Press provided support, encouragement, and editorial input. Special thanks go to the intrepid voyagers who left homes in the United States and came to Italy to share time with me there. I can never thank them enough for their belief in my writing and in Private Italy.

Always, my thanks go to my family and to Alan. They have believed in the dream from the very beginning and without them this journey would never have even begun.

Maps

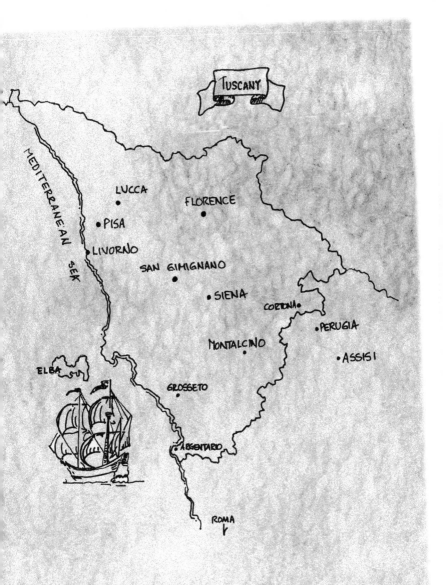

TUSCANY

MEDITERRANEAN SEA

LUCCA

FLORENCE

PISA

LIVORNO

SAN GIMIGNANO

SIENA

CORTONA

PERUGIA

MONTALCINO

ASSISI

ELBA

GROSSETO

ARGENTARIO

ROMA

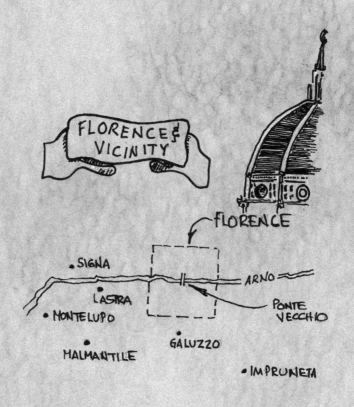

FLORENCE & VICINITY

FLORENCE

• SIGNA

ARNO

• LASTRA

PONTE VECCHIO

• MONTELUPO

• GALUZZO

• MALMANTILE

• IMPRUNETA

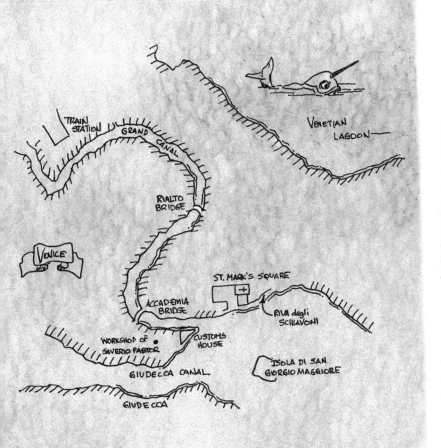

Tuscan Light

Prologue

Prologue

Florence. Snow falls on the ancient stones of the Ponte Vecchio. Predawn darkness wraps the city. Silence fills the squares and palaces of this most beloved of Italian cities. Along the edges of the river Arno, long fingers of snow beckon from marsh grasses. The city slumbers and is transformed into an engraving, light and dark, from decades long past.

I stroll down the long slope of the bridge and head toward the medieval center of the city. The large expanse of the Piazza della Signoria shows no footprint in the white blanket that smooths the worn stone pavement beneath. Wind whips between the loggia and columns of the Uffizi Gallery. A sheet of snow from atop the statue of David tumbles down onto the steps of the ancient palazzo and disappears into gathering drifting snow. This is my last morning here. My long and magical season is coming to a close.

When I arrived in the tiny village of Malmantile, spring leaves were reaching into a deep blue Tuscan sky. Blossom-covered olive trees and blue iris covered the hills above the Arno valley. The small villa that was to be my home for a season was located atop a hill on the outskirts of the village. Built around the walls of a thirteenth-century tower, it offered privacy, a retreat and a place from which to make new discoveries about the Italian people and their remarkable homeland.

This book of memories ranges freely over those changing seasons and locales. Malmantile, Florence, Venice, Rome—I share with you my impressions of Italy as I experienced them, in glimpses sometimes fleeting like snow, sometimes spread out like an alfresco feast on a summer day. You'll find no logical progression of plot here—but what you will find, I hope, is a rich assemblage of characters and settings, vignettes of people and places that make up a country unlike any other.

Snow gathers on my shoulders. I roll up the collar of my coat against the cold. At the conclusion of such a season, such a journey, there is a desire for more time, more places to see, more food and wine, more opportunities to observe the creation of objects inspired by great passions. I remember the kitchens of remarkable cooks, where simple recipes created unforgettable meals; the outdoor wood-burning oven of Janet and Stefano Magazzini where beefsteak, luscious and sweet, was served with hot crusted bread in the shade of a garden arbor; the taste of succulent red wines from the heart of Chianti; a late-night, high-water drift along the Grand Canal in Venice on a spring evening; the harvest of grapes and olives. The Italians have shown me the beautiful simplicity of their lives. The culture has come to life.

I turn and look high up against the facade of the Palazzo Vecchio—the ancient city hall. Its medieval tower is dusted, fragmented, by the falling snow. Light from a few windows in the palazzo illuminates the flakes as they pass by, golden-hued flashes against the deep dark shape of the building.

We come to understand a culture slowly, layer on layer. Experience by experience, the traditions are a living and natural outcome of how the people live—their food, their wine, what they love about place, their families, where their passions lie. In the midst of unprecedented change, including the introduction of the euro, can such a culture survive? Many Italians have shared with me that their greatest fear is the probable absorption of their ancient traditions into the "world culture," where rap music, immigration, and the pressures of global politics erode the uniqueness of Italian life. There is apprehension that what once was a distinctive and special way of life will eventually disappear. Profound changes may lie ahead, so remembering Italy as it is today becomes ever more important. With changes imminent, will Italy remain "Italian"?

The journey begins.

Places

Beginnings

The village of Malmantile flows over the top of a hill southwest of Florence, above the Arno-side town of Montelupo. I navigate the sharp twists and turns of the road as it curves up the hillside above the river. Small signs direct me through the heart of the village. The medieval fortress rises on my left. I pass the local alimentari (food shop), macelleria (butcher shop) and a café, holding my breath as the car squeezes by an old stone house on Via San Vito.

The car rumbles and groans as I negotiate a dusty, twisted, and rutted gravel road. Two large white dogs race from a fence-circled villa to bark a welcome as I pass. As I drive through a forest I begin to think that I have made a wrong turn. Not so. Just as I begin to seriously consider turning around and trying again, I come to a gate and find myself on the grounds of the villa. Two rows of umbrella pines (so named for their distinctly umbrella-like shape) line both sides of the road. As I park the car next to a small terrace an older woman peeks out of a doorway.

"Signor Smith?"

"Si. *Yes.*" I open the door of the car.

She smiles. "Benvenuto. I am Signora Bianca. Welcome to the villa."

"Grazie. It is good to be here."

I take my two suitcases from the car. She offers to help and I tell her that I have them, thanks all the same.

"Come." She holds a large key-laden iron ring in her hand. "I will show you the house and your room."

A terrace that fronts the villa faces east. On this splendid afternoon, the view is breathtaking. Warm afternoon sun fills the air. I look out over olive groves, their lush silver and green leaves fluttering in the breeze. Across the valley, vineyards line the way up to a golden-walled villa. Large rosemary plants border the outside perimeter of the terrace. Huge emerald-green cypress trees frame steps to the west side of the house.

"This is the living and dining room."

There is a fireplace at one end of the room. A thick wooden table with several chairs around it sits near an antique buffet. The portrait of a stern-faced cardinal faces out into the room from above the buffet—perhaps an ancestor of the family who has owned this villa for many generations.

The signora walks past the table and disappears into a hallway. I follow her in to the kitchen. She shows me a wooden cupboard full of dishes, cooking utensils, and pots along with a few food items purchased for my arrival. Light fills the room from an open window. A breeze stirs the trees outside.

In the course of the next few minutes she shows me my room, the bathroom, and the other small spaces of the building.

"Is there anything that I can get you before I leave?"

I stand in the center of the tiny library and wonder, *what more could I need?* "No, signora. I am fine. Thank you."

"You are most welcome. Until later, then."

She smiles and closes the main door behind her as she leaves. The villa falls silent.

After unpacking, I change into more comfortable clothes. Late afternoon light reminds me that the day will soon end. I take a chair up on a small rise of land on the south side of the house to view the sunset. Toward the west, the foothills above Pisa and Viareggio begin to fade dark green and purple as the sky moves through shades of blue to warm pink to darker blue. A chill begins to settle on the hills. I finally give in to weariness and re-enter the villa.

A light dinner of Tuscan dried ham (prosciutto), bread, and a bit of the local Chianti wine is followed by a warm shower. I open the shutters and windows of my room. As I slip into bed, an owl cries out from the distant hills. I turn off the lamp on my bedside table and fall quickly to sleep, held safely within the thick, ancient walls of this Tuscan home.

Villa Evening

Three lush lemon trees, in large terra cotta planters, line the north wall of the villa. The trees are full of large, plump fruit. A saucer of food and milk sits near one of the plants for Principessa, the local mouser cat. The cat is, according to the signora, "molto gravida," very pregnant. The signora always wears an apron, strong stout shoes, and a blouse with the sleeves rolled up. The cat rubs up against her leg.

There is majesty and elegance in the way the signora moves. She has worked, she says, almost every day since her husband died and left her nearly penniless. Faced with the reality of raising three sons with no income, she immediately sought work.

"The owners of this villa," she says, "gave me work. I have always been most grateful."

She rarely smiles, opting more often than not for a wonderful shrug of the shoulders and casual flip of her right hand.

"It has worked out well for you, then?" I reply.

"In somma." *In general.*

This particular evening, she postpones her normal schedule of after dinner cleaning to talk. Her beautiful brown eyes betray some spark of interest and curiosity.

"Why do you stay so long here? Why do you not live here?"

"Sometimes, Signora Bianca, it is enough to know that Italy, Tuscany, is here. When I return, the country and the people give so much. That is sufficient for now." I look out across the valley that fronts the terrace. "Italy is the most beautiful country on earth, I think." Her eyes are staring out across to the lights of a distant villa.

"Then why don't you stay permanently if it means so much to you?"

"Well, I have commitments back in America." My eyes meet hers. "But Tuscany, this country, never leaves my heart, mio cuore."

She wipes her nose with a blue handkerchief, quickly dabbing at her left eye. "An old injury," she mumbles. "It is sad to me that you cannot stay."

There is a faint scratching sound nearby. Principessa is stretching her claws on the base of a cypress tree. When I look up, the signora has started to walk back to her bicycle. The sun is beginning its final descent for the day. As she rattles by, pushing on the handlebars, she does something that she's never done before. She waves.

"Ciao, bello."

She puts her foot on the left pedal, raises her right foot through to the other side of the bike, and begins to ride down the path toward the forest's edge. I shout out, "Ciao bella, Signora!"

She is gone.

I turn away from the road and walk along the terrace. There is a *swoosh* above me. I look up just as a pair of bats streak across the opening between villa and cypress and then are gone. Far back behind me, an owl that I continue to hear in the evenings lets out a cry. The sunset breeze has died down. I take off my sandals and quietly walk down to a small pool near the house.

Dragonflies are gathered above the water. They dance in the golden light of sunset. I take a seat on the edge and slowly lower my feet into the cool water. Occasionally a car across the valley makes its presence known by the rub of tires on pavement. A bat appears and slips along the surface of the water for a drink, startling the dragonflies.

Night descends on this hilltop of Tuscany. Predators seek their prey. The air stills and settles on trees that will be, by morning, wet with dew. Across this small valley, Signora Bianca finds rest in the shelter of her home.

"Dormire bene." *Sleep well.*

Fog

The hills south of the villa are covered in vineyards. Sangiovese grapes, the backbone of Chianti, hang within the rising brown arms of the vine. There is increasingly excited talk about the upcoming season. Will the grapes ripen early? Will they produce a fine harvest?

This is early spring. Dense fog often covers the hills of Tuscany at this time of year. On this early morning, I am walking between rows of vines. Cool veils of mist wet my skin as a small rabbit skitters across the path. It leaves no trace as it disappears up ahead of me. I've heard an owl in the pine forest on recent evenings and it is no wonder that the rabbit moves with such intense purpose. Not me. I walk slowly, taking in the feel of the earth beneath my feet, and the cool cloud that covers the vineyard.

As the sun rises above the crest of the hill, twisted and gnarled branches of vines reach out menacingly from the mist. I hear voices from behind me. The workers are out early, preparing the soil, tending the vines. Ghosts of the land, of laborers from ages past, whisper around me from the fog.

These lands have been tended since the fourteenth century. With the help of Valambrosian monks, a noble Tuscan family began to work the land in the hopes that it would support the growth of grape and olive. Their work succeeded; for over five hundred years the grapes have given life and heart to the great wines of Chianti. The monks moved on, in 1598, to join another group of their order near Gaiole in Chianti. From that time on the responsibility for the growth and produce of the vines rested squarely on the shoulders of the landholders.

The workmen's voices echo through the fog. Branches brush my hands and arms, reaching out from the mist as if asking for alms, some gift to alleviate the possibility of a poor harvest, some guarantee of success.

Up ahead a worker suddenly appears, at first a frightening vision.

"Buongiorno, Signor Smith!"

It is Giovanni, one of the workers I have seen pruning the olive trees. We speak for a few moments, concentrating our discussion on the vines, the weather.

"Il tempo oggi fare bene per uve," he says. *Today's weather bodes well for the grapes.* I smile.

"Speriamo," I reply. *I hope.*

We shake hands as he scoots by me, both of us brushing against the branches of the vines.

He disappears into the fog, the vines directing his walk down to his labor somewhere with the other workers. A patch of blue appears overhead. I have arrived at the farthest edge of the vineyard. The sun breaks through. The fog begins to lift, one large sheet of mist that undulates above the vines, thinning as it slowly disappears into a clear, bright morning sky.

The other workers who stand surprisingly close are gathered around Giovanni as they discuss the day's work. Back down by the villa, Signora Bianca talks to her sons who stand in rapt attention as she doles out the day's work on the olive trees. I overhear her talking about the olive grove. In the spring of each year, the olive trees must be pruned of their unnecessary growth. Each man nods in concentrated agreement as she talks. One slumps with hands in pockets, staring at the ground. Another doesn't take his eyes off of "Mama," and another waves at my approach.

A number of trees have been pruned, the twigs and unneeded branches stacked in open spaces around the groves. These "suckers," as they are called, are cut away to allow for more sunlight on the best-producing branches of the trees. One of the signora's sons moves with purpose down the hill towards a pile of these branches. I know that soon the twigs that once reached up through the cold sky and air of a Tuscan winter will be consumed by the fires of spring. He pours fuel over the branches, reaches into his pocket, and pulls out a box of matches. He strikes one, steps away from the pile, and tosses the lighted match into the branches. They whoosh to flame. The branches crackle and snap in the early morning air. Smoke occludes the sun as it rises further in the morning sky.

The signora watches, arms folded, as her sons go to their labor. One son stands by the fires in the olive grove. Another drives a tractor across the rough land to begin the pruning process on trees farther away from the villa. A third walks among the vines, checking the grapes as he goes. The muted conversations of workers in the vineyard, once overpowered by a noisy tractor, again fill the air.

Signora Bianca waves for me to join her. "I am so very proud of my sons, and of this land." She wipes her hands on her apron. "Families have worked this land for many centuries. We do what we can. So it goes." She walks back into her working room at the back of the villa.

For centuries, hands have tended these trees and vines. Olive and grape receive equally passionate, caring attention. Whether every member of a family, or the laborers, live to taste the results of their work seems immaterial; what matters is the tradition of bounty from the land and knowledge that life, as in nature, turns year on year. A drop of golden oil, or the luscious flavor of an aged Chianti wine, tell the story best. Were it not for such love of the land, for time and the vagaries of fickle nature, life in Italy would be so different. How fortunate for those who work the land to understand their responsibility; what a gift to those of us who enjoy the fruits of their labors, and those of past generations.

Shadows

S undays at the villa are the most restful, quiet, and inspiring days of my time here. Signora Bianca abandons her daily vigil of cleaning and cooking to attend to family and her own errands in the village. The noise of the clunky old diesel tractor doesn't intrude on the silence. Birds quietly fly from olive tree to olive tree and, in the rising heat, shadows stand out against the roughest of clay soil.

Up in the vineyards, hundreds of brilliant green serrated leaves on grapevines flutter in the breeze. A few rabbits from the woods occasionally appear, flashing in and out of the vineyard's shadows. In the thicket of nearby shrubs, crickets drone as the heat rises.

Such quiet encourages exploration of the villa. Early in the thirteenth century, Signora Bianca says, warring factions shed blood along roads connecting Florence, Prato, Pisa, and other cities across Italy. Fortifications were built for both defensive and warning purposes. Fires were lit from atop towers to warn others of marching armies. Such was the case with the first tower built on this land.

The oldest part of the villa, built in the thirteenth century, is now a small den. There is a black iron ring centered in the ceiling. The ring was used to steady animals in what once was a stable. The body heat from the cows and horses provided warmth to those who lived in the rooms above. A wood-framed window in the den stands open. The view out over freshly cut grass, through a stand of umbrella pine trees, beckons. A breeze softly whispers into the room. The sense of calm and serenity is wonderful. No feeling of the early days of bloodshed remains. What was left behind by those earliest inhabitants? Perhaps the spirit of a protective soul.

There is a small table centered on the large, rarely used fireplace in the den. One evening I flipped up the corner of the table's cloth cover and placed a small vase on the folded cloth as a reminder. I needed to ask Signora Bianca about firewood. I then headed up to bed. The windows in the den were closed, and the flue on the fireplace was shut tight.

When I returned in the morning, the windows were shut, the flue still closed. The vase, however, was in the center of the coffee table, and the turned-back corner of fabric had been smoothly flattened back in place. The hair on my arms stood up. I sensed something, someone, in the empty room. The next evening I did the same thing with the vase and the corner of the cloth. The next morning, the same result.

This ancient tower must contain within its walls the

echoes of war, as well as the remnants of human existence. It seems to me that the spirit, or spirits, that inhabit the villa must have good reason to be here. The shadows that move through this house must enjoy being where they are, in a lovingly restored building perched high on a hill between Prato and Florence. Only the occasional intrusion of trespassers like us interrupts their long evening walks through the rooms.

The huge shutter-framed windows on the west wall of the house open to a view across a rich green valley and olive grove. Beyond are the red-tiled rooftops of Prato. Beyond that city, the hazy presence of the mountains of Carrara (where Michelangelo often selected blocks of marble) is outlined against a cerulean sky. The rising heat causes the distant mountains to shimmer. A bird in the pine trees just outside the window calls into the olive grove and another, far away, replies. I turn, leave the main room through the double-arched wood doors, and take a seat at the terrace table.

An old, bent pine tree arches over the terrace. It has been propped up with a kind of crutch. One large knot in the tree looks, in the long afternoon light, like the face of an old man. Perhaps this is a way for the spirits of the house to remind me that they are here. The shade of the tree provides relief from the warmth of the day. I continue to write as quiet settles on the grounds of the villa.

I can only imagine the changes such a place has seen. The fortress of Malmantile was built in the fourteenth century. Church emissaries, traveling from Rome to cities in the North, once crossed this land. In the mid-fifteenth century, the Medici dynasty in Florence established itself as the premier banking power of the Italian Renaissance. Troops from around the world struggled across these hills during two world wars. Kings and queens, princes and their courts, and presidents came to power and, soon enough, were replaced.

Up on this peaceful hill there is little remaining of all that history. Men and women come and go, and some of their shadows remain to protect this place. I've come to accept that such spirits truly do exist. On Sunday morning, especially, when there are no interruptions of manmade noise, even the slow pace of farm life in Tuscany comes nearly to a halt. The muses awake. Pen finds paper, and a certain shadow leans over my shoulder to whisper continued words of encouragement and inspiration.

Veils of Gamberaia

Tuscany and gardens fit together naturally—seven letters, equal partners. Villa Gamberaia and its gardens have been famous for centuries. The beauty of the villa's location and the variety of plantings draw garden architects from around the globe. Horticulturists come to study the seeming ease with which this marvelous place—parterre, cypress hedges, water iris—are all precisely set into a glorious high terrace near the small hill town of Settignano, above Florence.

Among the owners of the Gamberaia, none is more curious or famous than Princess Ghinka. She was a young woman when she acquired the villa. In 1896, the open spaces around the villa were simple, nondescript spaces of green. She gave them color and light. A singularly reclusive woman, she brought a lover into her life and for most of their years together (she an Albanian, her lover an Italian of illustrious descent) they inhabited the villa, rarely leaving the confines of their rooms except at night.

In the approaching darkness the princess, also rumored to have been self-consciously unattractive, would emerge from her rooms. Draped in veils to hide her form and figure, she would wander through the rose garden and water-dappled parterre. Servants told others of her solitary walks: a white-veiled apparition slowly coursing through the garden on moonless nights, her hands caressing the boxwood hedges as she strolled through the water garden and disappeared into the cypress hedges beyond.

She worked with several garden architects to perfect work begun by previous owners. Villa Gamberaia is now judged the most splendid garden in all of Tuscany. From the unlimited vistas over the valley of the Arno River and Florence to the olive tree–covered hills surrounding the villa, there is never a bad view. The water garden blossoms with deep blue iris and water lilies in the spring. Lemon trees stand throughout the garden. Peppermint-scented geraniums flow gently over terra cotta pots. Cypress hedges in the form of arches line much of the garden. Roses bloom and perfume the air. Scents blend with vistas.

Over the decades that followed Princess Ghinka's death, a legend grew. For as many times as the villa traded hands—once even occupied by the German army during the Second World War—stories circulated about the apparition of a veiled princess. Visitors reported seeing her on moonless nights spiriting between hedges and lemon trees. The stories persist to this day.

The current owners of the villa offer rental apartments in two of the property's buildings. I have rented one of them. On a moonless August night, the princess does not disappoint. As evening approaches, the bells of Settignano echo across the garden. A gentle breeze stirs the trees and hedges. The sun sets. The curtain of night, a purple line that slowly floats overhead on its way west, brings a quiet, blue-hued mist to the garden. On the grove-covered hills, an owl cries out into the night and a bat flutters across the archway of cypresses.

As I stroll in the gardens after sunset, I turn a corner onto the bowling green, a dramatic greenway that stretches north across the expanses of lawn and plantings. I notice a form—a shadow really—against the balustrade underneath a huge pine tree at the edge of the garden. It is difficult to make out if it is a man or a woman. There is only the sense of a person, an outlined shadow that does not move. A noise distracts my attention. When I again look toward the balustrade, the shadow is gone. I walk to where the form had been and there is no sign of anyone. I turn to leave, and then hear it—the faint rustle of clothing against shrubbery and the soft clap of feet on cool earth. It sounds as if someone is walking through the arched cypress loggia. I follow the sound.

The breeze across the hills quiets to a whisper. I continue to follow the sound of someone walking, always a few feet ahead of me. The scent of roses surrounds me. The shadow weaves temptingly in and out of sight, allowing only an occasional glimpse, further confounding my sense of belief. When I reach the small garden gate, near lemon trees neatly arranged in planters, the shadow slips quickly around the corner of the secret garden.

I pause. Could I have imagined this? The sound of a crash breaks my reverie and I rush into the garden. On the pavement, near the fountain at the far end of the garden, I discover a terra cotta planter shattered beneath a high balcony. When I look up, a white veil slowly recedes from the high balustrade, and the muffled sound of a sigh echoes softly in the air. I stoop to collect bits and pieces of the clay; the flowers are moved into the grass until morning. When I rise back up to leave the garden, I notice something hanging from the hand of a large statue near the entrance gate. I approach and slowly lift a small torn fragment of a veil from the hand and stare at it in disbelief.

Gardens of inexorable beauty have a way of getting under your skin, of never leaving your mind, of becoming a place of refuge when you get home. In the days of winter, memories of Tuscany's gardens provide respite from the cold, frozen hours that come. So it is with the night that a princess appeared in the shadows of the garden at Villa Gamberaia, a place protected forever by her spirit.

That small piece of veil remains with me to this day.

The N Line

Vaporetti, the water buses of Venice, course the water of the Venetian lagoon deep into the night. The night schedule of the vaporetti is known as the "N" schedule. I board one of these floating buses on the Grand Canal near the train station.

Away from the bright lights of the piazza that fronts the station, the city walls, dark and ominous, appear above water as smooth and silvery as mercury. We float past great gray ghosts of churches. Large phenomenal shapes, carved from some sculptor's vision, cast high shadows against arched marble.

A full moon pulls the tide achingly high. Boats, tied to the shore, bow low in the water. Some appear close to sinking. Another vaporetto appears along our right side, a lead-colored reflected vision that moves ahead of us, spirit-like. Light from the linen-white moon illuminates the reflection of the boat in the canal. In windows high above the canal, candlelight warms the walls within palazzos. The great expanses of facades that line the canal are interrupted, here and there, by smaller waterways. They offer tempting glimpses of Venice's darker shadows, places into which, from our route on the N line, we are not permitted to see.

Venice doesn't live in sunlight. When the throngs of people who fill these canals with the necessary commerce of the city are all gone, Venice groans back to its true life. Tourists with their hopes have made this city what they think it should be, not what it is. In the midst of Venetian nights, masked ghosts appear in the windows. The ephemeral voices of the doges who once governed the Venetian republic whisper around the arches of palazzos. Ghosts of dead lovers gather again to stand in dark corners along the canal, wistfully and silently watching as mortals float past.

This is their city. We interlopers breathe the air in which they lived. With a longing smile, they flick a small particle of dust from a tomb, or a fleck of history from atop an old monument. We inhale it, and it stays with us for the rest of our lives. The particle lodges in our souls and when the simple word "Venice" comes to us, we remember a night such as this.

The vaporetto that once led us down the canal has moved on. We approach the huge bend in the canal near the Rialto Bridge, a signature white confection of an arch that marks the midpoint on the canal. A luminous display of candles has been lit along the canal near a palazzo. Their fire flickers against the gargoyles and twisted columns of the ancient stones. I look up just in time to see the full moon blink between the facade of a palazzo and the great bridge.

As we follow the curve of the canal past the Accademia museum, the Customs House comes into view. The Palazzo Dario, the most infamous of Venice's palazzos, leans precariously away from the Palazzo de Venier dei Leoni (home of the Peggy Guggenheim Collection). The stories of tragedy and death that have haunted the Palazzo Dario's owners remain the talk of Venice; suicides, murders and terrible accidents have befallen all who have attempted to possess it. As I look high up along its facade, I imagine great wraiths who have attempted to corrupt such splendor, and then fled in frustration over their inability to pierce the beauty of this floating city. Death may come to those unfortunate few, yet the beauty of Venice triumphs.

The vaporetto at long last arrives at the San Zaccaria stop, near Saint Mark's Square. I disembark. A few people still stroll through the grand expanse of the Piazza San Marco. There are several flagpoles in front of the Basilica of Saint Mark. They are topped with resplendent gold lions, the symbol of Venice. At night, narrow beams of light illuminate each of them. I look up at their beauty, contrasted against the dome of darkness that covers Venice this night. Such is this city, a place that shines out against all of the other cities in the world—baffling, confounding, mystical, and romantic.

It is far past midnight. I return to my hotel for a night's rest. Sunrise will come early tomorrow. I wish to see light rise above this implausible city.

Sunrise

It is still dark when I rouse from sleep. The air is damp and heavy. I walk out onto the balcony of my room, a cup of fresh coffee in hand, and take in one of the most famous views in the world. The Riva degli Schiavoni is an expansive walkway of stone that begins near the Piazza San Marco. Throngs of visitors seek out this famous pedestrian area during the day. They come to enjoy views across the waterway known as the Canale di San Marco. On this early morning, the Riva is nearly empty.

Only the slightest traces of light hint along the eastern horizon, out past the island of the Lido. Boats float by on a coal-black sea. Some are large and well lit; others carry only a small red light to negotiate the canals. San Giorgio Maggiore, the marvelous cathedral designed by Palladio, looms in the distance across the canal. A few lights illuminate some details of the church and monastery. The large tower and dome loom into dark skies above.

A cart is wheeled into a corner near the San Zaccaria vaporetto stop, its wheels squeaking and groaning under the owner's struggle to move it into position. He unlocks a few padlocks and begins to open the stall in preparation for the day's work. A foghorn moans into the early morning air. A dove arrives at my feet, cooing and looking around nervously. The sun continues to slowly lighten the eastern sky.

Santa Maria della Salute, another enormous cathedral farther up the Grand Canal, begins to glow, suffused by a pink light that somehow grows more iridescent as the sun rises into morning. A gondolier, straw hat perched securely on his head, walks by. He chats quietly on a cell phone. Seagulls cry in the distance or flutter by overhead, swift, silent messengers of the waking day.

Two men strain to move a large flat cart loaded with bright yellow plastic containers full of bottled water across the stones of the Riva. They haul the cart over to a nearby barge. Other workers rapidly load the bottles onto their boat. A few birds gather around the workmen, seeking a small treat. Gondolas along the canal, brought here empty from corners across the city, are guided to their platforms by jacketed gondoliers. The boats bob and float in a small harbor that fronts the Palazzo Ducale, once home to the governing councils of the city. The large, silver-tipped tails of these signature boats catch the sun and flash morning light against the sea.

Far across the Giudecca Canal the Redentore church (Church of the Redeemer), with its glorious white marble facade, begins to glow light orange and pink. Its high dome, protected by two pencil-thin towers, brightens to a light gray, outlined by a violet background. The surface of the canals glistens as the sky continues to brighten. The vaporetti that come and go are filled with morning commuters. A bright streak of sunlight released between clouds from far out above the Adriatic strikes the campanile (bell tower) of San Giorgio Maggiore. Birds rise to the light. The tower glows saffron and green, its copper-topped belfry abruptly awakened by this glorious burst of light. Large dark-blue barges cut back and forth in the canal carrying the day's goods to businesses throughout the city.

The hotel, terrace and all, seems to float into the sea. The subtle sway of so many boats makes me believe that the entire city ebbs and flows, that it all rocks gently back and forth to some unheard Venetian song. Cobalt blue striped boats share the canal with the vaporetti. Forsythia-yellow vessels slip next to docks, their colors reflecting into the sea, creating an ever-changing mosaic. Deep green barges carrying the necessary supplies of the city float past the vaporetti. It is cacophonous, splendid, and unforgettable.

The sun finally rises above the rooftops of the Lido. The canal is bathed in light. I count no fewer than twenty different boats now cutting across the canal. More stalls on the broad walkway in front of the hotel are opened for business.

The day begins.

Across this great wide globe, there is only one city afloat on the seas, only one place where the moon pulls waters closer to its light in a way that makes boats bend, only one incredible, ineffable, indefinable, nearly unimaginable place. Venice.

Badia

Valambrosian monks established a monastery on a high and remote Italian hillside some seventy miles south of Florence. It was there, in the eleventh century, that they laid the cornerstone of what became the Badia a Coltibuono. Their buildings were constructed from dark gray stone, quarried from the mountains upon which they lived. Vines were planted in the rough soil. Thanks to the tender care of the grapes, viticulture was born in what is now the Classico region of Tuscany. The monks prospered and purchased large tracts of land upon which to plant more vines.

In 1810, Napoleon's troops occupied the Badia. The monks were forced to flee. The property was secularized, and then sold off to various owners. In the nineteenth century the land and buildings were purchased by Guido Giunti. It has remained in the family ever since.

Visitors to this private, family-held estate discover a place of tranquility. Guido's great-grandson, Piero Stucchi-Prunetti, married Lorenza de Medici. Her numerous cookbooks and cooking lessons breathed new life into Tuscan cooking. It is their children who continue to manage the day-to-day operations of the property. My first encounter with Guido Stucchi-Prunetti, one of Lorenza's sons, occurs in the spring.

I arrive at the Badia (pronounced Bah-*dee*-ah), on a late April morning, eager to learn more about the estate's wine and olive production. A rising mist blankets the stone walls at the main entrance and holds fast along the narrow winding road that brings me to my first view of the buildings on the estate. Fog whispers around the vineyards. Spring green leaves hold the promise of a new season. A dog barks off in the distance as a squirrel runs across the graveled walkway. I make my way up to two towering oak doors built into the lichen-covered walls of the ancient abbey. I ring the bell promptly at nine and await Guido's arrival. A car pulls up the gray-graveled drive and a young man bursts from the car and strides toward me.

"Buongiorno," he says, smiling.

"Buongiorno, Signore. I have an appointment with Guido Stucchi this morning."

"I am Guido." He shakes my hand and smiles. Keys rattle in his hand as he opens one of the gates.

The main courtyard is paved in rain-polished stones. Through an archway on the far side of the square I can see arbors of a large garden. A large white dog lies up against one of the walls in the courtyard. Guido strides ahead to a glass side door near the gate.

"Here is our office. Please come in." The warm interior

takes the chill off the morning mist and he graciously offers a coffee.

"Grazie."

Our meeting takes only a half hour. As we talk, I study Guido's face. Deep in the past generations of this family runs the blood of the Medici, the most famous of numerous political families who governed Renaissance Florence. Bright eyes and a quiet, confident demeanor lie beneath his poised and well-tailored presence. He is animated, accommodating, and genial. He offers to continue our discussion during a tour of the monastery and gardens. As we leave the office, a large, dark brown dog rises from across the courtyard and barks at our approach. The white dog stirs and joins the uproar.

A window opens up in one of the buildings that face the courtyard. A young boy, perhaps aged six, leans out above us. It looks like a painting: rough, hand-cut stones form a contrasting window frame. Shutters flank the window. The boy has dark hair, dark eyes—a noble figure even at such a young age.

"Babbo," he asks. *Father.* "Why the noise?"

"It is nothing. Go back inside. Get ready for school."

The boy disappears. Glass panes glint against the sun as the window latch scrapes shut. Guido leads me into a sun-filled hallway. We walk to a pair of open doors. He leads me down into the shadowy, ancient cellar. Great oak casks, some of them full of wine, line both sides of the underground room. It smells of must and earth.

"Some of our wine," he explains, "ages in these French oak casks. We do not have space for all of it here. Most is stored at our winery several kilometers from here."

Guido's pride is evident. "All of our olive oils and wines are produced, and bottled, on our land." He pauses and places a hand on the tap of one of these huge oak casks.

"'Coltibuono' means 'of the good harvest,'" Guido continues. "We try to keep the centuries of tradition alive in every bottle of wine we produce."

The arched passageway narrows as we walk past walls covered in dark mold. He explains that I should avoid touching it and adds that the mold is a necessary by-product of the cellar's constant temperature and age. I suddenly find that we are standing in a space where all four walls are lined with dust-covered bottles. Above many of the rows are signs that indicate the year of production; the oldest dates back to 1936.

"This is our family's private cellar," he says. "Once in a great while we take out a bottle and enjoy the work of generations past. We also check the vintages when required. It is our own small treasure."

Guido leads me up a set of steep stairs and into a beautiful room. "This is the refectory, the room where the monks would eat," he tells me. Large stucco arches reach high above us. The walls glow with frescoes.

"Just before Napoleon occupied the Badia in the early 1800s, the monks covered all of the frescoes." He waves his hand in a circular motion around the room. "Whitewash, rather than paint, was deliberately used to paint over them. This made their restoration much easier."

Centered in one of the arches directly above us, he points out, is the coat of arms of the Badia. It shows the hand of a monk atop the handle of a shovel, uniting them with the earth, a wreath of olive leaves to symbolize redemption, and the ladder of Saint Lawrence (upon which the saint was burned alive), reminding all of sacrifice.

White cotton-covered chairs and sofas contrast with a burnished grand piano. An elegant arrangement of lilies and other spring flowers sits atop a large round oak table. Bright morning light enters through large glass doors through which I can see the garden.

"Come. I will show you where our cooking lessons take place." He holds the door for me as I enter a large terra cotta–tiled kitchen. Numerous copper pots and pans hang from racks around the room and above the counters. A large butcher-block table surrounded by stools makes it abundantly clear that this is a place of work and learning. A shaft of morning light illuminates a large stove and work counter.

"My mother, Signora de Medici, used to lead her cooking classes here. Now others lead groups through the classes."

I imagine the work that takes place here—the joyous, sensual craft of creating luscious meals from flour, salt, pepper, cheeses, chicken, beef, fish, and fresh vegetables—the list is nearly endless. Trace odors of garlic, warm bread, and spices still suffuse the air.

As we leave the kitchen and stroll onto the gravel pathways of the garden, Guido explains that a few years ago, his brother, Paolo, transformed what had been the carriage house and stables of the estate into a restaurant. "You should eat there," he suggests to me.

My mind tries to imagine what it must be like to live in such a place. The extraordinary responsibilities of their work underscore how much passion Signora de Medici, her husband and, subsequently, her children have for the work of the vine, the olive, and great food.

"Would you like to see the restaurant? You must meet Paolo."

The fog has lifted and a slight breeze hints of a clear, bright day ahead. We stroll to the restaurant. It is off to the side of the main building complex. Several tables are placed outside on three large terraces that step down a hillside. The view of the valley below the Badia is spectacular. We enter the main bar area of the restaurant and a dark, imposing man walks up.

"Ciao." He looks at me and extends his hand.

Guido introduces me to Paolo, and at Paolo's urging he and I sit at the bar for an espresso. Paolo works at the espresso machine and produces three cups of frothy black brew. He stands behind the bar, hands spread wide on the tiled surface. The space has been beautifully transformed from its earlier function. Light golden-colored stucco covers the walls. Deep red terra cotta tiles shine on the floor and the entire east wall of the space is lined with huge glass windows. Light comes into the room from beneath the outdoor rose trellis.

Paolo hands me a menu. It is clear that the chef has dedicated a great deal of time to produce a delicious variety of courses. A sample: local cold cuts and a selection of warm croutons; homemade short pasta with aubergine ragout and anchovies; veal shank braised in Sangiovese grapes and served with sautéed fennel; dark chocolate cake with candied lemon. I thank Paolo and shake hands, telling him that I look forward to returning for a meal in the near future.

The white dog from the courtyard slowly saunters up to Guido as we approach the family chapel. He reaches down and pets the dog. The gravel crunches beneath our shoes. A few birds circle overhead. Steam rises from the stone wall as the sun warms up a splendid spring day.

"We do love our work here. There are days, as anywhere, where we feel stress, but then we drink a glass of our Chianti and troubles flee."

We shake hands.

"A dopo." *Until later.*

"Si, a dopo." *See you again soon.* Guido turns and disappears behind the great oak gates of the courtyard.

The bell tower of the Badia chapel rises next to me. I stop for a few moments to take in the view. Water drips from the trees onto the pavement behind me. Steam continues to rise from a low stone wall in front of me. A few remnants of fog glide by overhead. I drive back down the twisting road to the highway and return to Florence.

When I think back to that spring morning, I remember three things: the deep affection and appreciation the family has for their history; the care given to the products produced on the estate; and the richness of the land. Were it not for the land those ancient monks sweated and toiled over, the grapes of Chianti would surely have grown somewhere else. How fortunate for all that places like the Badia—the Abbey—exist.

Blue Where They Fell

A sky of burnished gold rises above the shaded streets of Assisi. An older woman, stooped over a broom, quietly sweeps the night's dust from the stones in front of her store. The Via Fontabella, a narrow road that fronts the Hotel Giotto, angles steeply down to the junction of Piazza San Pietro (Square of Saint Peter) and the Porta di San Francesco (City gate of Saint Francis). At this early hour, the streets are almost deserted. My approach to the Basilica of Saint Francis takes me along the Via Frate Elia into the square below the cathedral. The morning sun reflects off of stained glass windows in the church and turns the center of the square into a mosaic of reds, blues, and greens.

The massive, high doors to the lower transept of the church are closed against the rising light of morning. There is a sudden loud thud, followed by the sound of metal on stone. Slowly, ever so slowly, the huge wooden doors to the lower entrance of the basilica begin to open. Two monks, side by side, methodically shuffle their sandaled feet as one door, and then another, is opened to the day. The glorious light of an Umbrian morning once more illuminates the patterned floor of the church. I walk up the long ramp that leads to the main entrance to the cathedral and approach one of the guards at the doors.

"Will Mass will be given today in the upper church?"

"There will be a Mass at six this afternoon in the lower transept of the church. Only then. Not now." He glances over my shoulder and nods at someone coming up behind me. I thank him and enter the church.

Work on this great edifice was started only two years after the death of Saint Francis, founder of the Franciscan monastic order. His remains now rest in a small crypt under the lower church. For more than 750 years this building has withstood the tests of time, war, and plague. Up high in the arches of the church are frescoes created by Giotto, one of the greatest artists of the early Renaissance. The ceiling above the main altar and back toward the front entrance to the church is a field of deep blue frescoes studded with gold stars.

An earthquake trembled across the valley below Assisi in September of 1997. It nearly destroyed the town of Foligno and took its toll on many other Umbrian cities and villages, Assisi included. Two priests, and two other men, were standing in the cathedral at almost the exact spot where I stand this morning. A strong aftershock rocked the cathedral. The ceiling above them gave way. They all perished in a dust cloud of ancient brick, stucco and fresco.

A monk smiles and stops nearby.

"May I help answer a question?"

"Yes. Thank you. Were you here the day of the . . . ?" My voice trails off.

"Oh, yes," he replies. He rubs his forehead and shifts his sandals against the skin-smooth surface of the floor. "Yes," he says again as he lowers his head. "They were blue where they fell." He looks up at me.

"I am not sure I understand."

He smiles again.

"The frescoes. As you can see,"—his hand sweeps above us to the ceiling—"most of them are painted with a dark blue background. When I entered the church only hours after the accident, the piles of rubble, especially here"—he makes a circular motion with his hand around us—"where we lost our friends, was covered in a sea of blue." He rubs his jaw.

I begin to comprehend the scene, terrible and quiet.

"The frescoes were blue where they fell. There are a number of rooms in this complex where those frescoes are being put back together, piece-by-piece—a huge project." He pulls up the sleeve of his robe and glances at his watch. "Oh, I must go."

"Yes, of course."

He turns and walks towards the main altar.

"Thank you," I offer.

His brown robes float around him as he waves and disappears behind a door. I walk over, stand directly below the crossed arched vaults and peer up into the immense open space. Cobalt blue frescoes fill each quarter of the high arches in the cathedral. Gold stars shine out from against the background. Imagining the force of the earthquake is beyond my comprehension. The time it will take to repair the damaged frescoes will be counted in decades, perhaps centuries.

Most art experts agree that from A.D. 1290 to 1295 a young Giotto and his assistants created these twenty-eight luminous frescoes depicting the life of Saint Francis. The art work covers the north and south interior walls of the cathedral.

I wonder if Giotto could have imagined that his vision of Saint Francis would last so many centuries. Certainly he could not have known that when nature conspired to shake his works from the interior skin of this cathedral, some of the frescoes would be blue where they fell.

Chance Meetings

Heat rises from the large open square that fronts the train station in Venice. Weary visitors lounge on the white marble terrace; some lean against the five broad marble stairs, resting on both elbows, legs extended lazily on the steps below. Confused and frazzled new arrivals squint into the bright afternoon sun, not quite sure how to absorb the view before them. Near a ticket window for the water buses, the vaporetti, a man yells out in English, Italian, French, German and (I believe) Japanese, "Venice maps. Venice maps."

In the corner of the square, a group of South American Indians has set up three microphones. Black speakers face out into the crowds. The musicians' bodies are covered in paint.

White stripes cross their bare chests and arms. Feathers stick out from behind their headbands. They all wear Nike sandals. Their music begins, filling the space across this broad expanse of the Grand Canal, echoing off the walls of churches and hotels. Pan pipes are the instrument of choice, along with a flute and some bongo drums. The beat is a mix of reggae meets flamenco meets jazz. Curious Chinese visitors gather in front of the players and take photos. Japanese tourists float by in gondolas, listening to the music as they gape in awe at this most incredible of cities. People from Bombay mix with college kids from Kansas as perplexed Italians stare in head-shaking resignation.

As I make my way to the Piazza San Marco onboard a vaporetto, visitors' languages from around the world blend together. Laughter interrupts the conversations around me. Smiles abound and people ask each other, sometimes in an ad-lib sign language, where something is, what stop to get off the water bus, or answer the easy question, "Where are you from?"

A gentleman whom I guess to be from India walks up to me to ask a question. He smiles and, in perfect British-accented English, asks which stop to use for the Church of Santa Maria della Salute. We consult my small map and I show him where he needs to disembark.

He smiles. "Thank you. Where are you from?"

"The States."

White teeth gleam from his open smile.

"And you?" I ask.

"Oh," he moves his head and neck in a sensuous curve, "we are from Mumbai (Bombay)." He nods in the direction of a group of friends standing along the rail of the vaporetto.

"Ah. What brings you here?"

"We are on a pilgrimage of sorts, to visit the churches of Europe. The university where we work at home supported our inquiries."

His phrasing sounds as stiffly British as any Englishman's.

"How long have you been in Europe?" I inquire.

"For thirty days. This is our last city. My friends and I go to Frankfurt tomorrow, for a day, before we fly back home."

We stroll across the deck of the boat as we continue our conversation. "What have you learned?" I ask him.

"It is confusing, I must say."

"How so?"

"We have so many gods in India. Our religious belief is such that each living being is blessed, and the gods of the water, the sky and the air all have their role in helping us make our way." He pauses to take a photo of a palace along the canal. "It seems to me that only one god is an interesting idea. While I understand the concept, it is difficult to accept. Look at that!" He points across the canal to the facade of a huge white palace. A few seagulls float past us above the canal.

My new friend continues. "The earth is far more complex than only one god could handle, we believe. Here, where the water and the stone fight for space, where the air blends with the buildings, our gods are working, fighting their jealousies, and struggling to sustain the world." He pauses. "Do you understand what I am saying?"

"Yes." I nod. "I'm thinking. Have you enjoyed seeing the churches and the places you've visited?"

"Oh, yes, very much. We chose to end our trip in Venice, as we had heard, rightfully so, that this is a place of incredible beauty. We find it astounding."

"This is your stop."

Our vaporetto is tied up to a floating dock along the canal, near the church he has asked about earlier.

"Oh, well then, I must go." Again, he makes that curve of the neck and head in a sinuous wave. "I apologize."

"For what?" I ask.

"For talking quite too much. Thank you. I have enjoyed our conversation."

He gives me a wide smile, shakes my hand and joins his group as they leave the boat. The boat pulls away from the dock.

His words haunt me. His view of the earth, of the city of Venice, is so different from mine. How difficult, indeed, it must be to transition between cultures as they have done. Boarding a plane in Mumbai, they fly for hours across a globe unmarked by borders and see it as a place where their gods constantly struggle to keep it all in balance. When you get right down to it, most of our spiritual beliefs fit such a vision: trying to keep it all in balance.

I leave the vaporetto at San Zaccaria, near Piazza San Marco. Groups of Americans listen to a guide, while various clusters of French, Chinese, Indian, and Spanish tourists all view the Church of San Marco, and the splendid Piazza that fronts it, through their own eyes.

What a blend, what a world. South American natives, dressed like western American Indians, play music on Greek pan flutes while people from all over the world listen. A new kind of world culture is creating itself. The lines that once separated one way of life from another have started to blur. We are swept up in the process of change. Indians who come to Europe, to the west, to learn of a religion where only one God oversees all, share thoughts with visitors from half a world away. Our perspective of the world is forever altered by those conversations. Chance meetings on a vaporetto with a man or woman we will not meet again, get under our skin and we can never be the same again. No longer clearly American, English, Russian, or Egyptian, we begin to see ourselves as being from the Earth, from the place we all, ultimately, call our home.

Bellinis at Harry's

On an unusually cold, damp September afternoon, I decide to slip into Harry's Bar in Venice. Steps from the "grandest salon in Europe," Saint Mark's Square, the bar has become a beacon to the tourist who desires a piece, a taste of more modern Italian history. We all want to be in a place known by Hemingway, Capote, Sartre, Picasso, Piaf and Loren. All summed up? The Bellini, a drink invented in this bar.

Comfortably seated in a corner of this incredibly small bar, I gain the waiter's attention. It is far too noisy to be heard above the raucous mix of conversation and laughter. The waiter mouths the word "Bellini." I nod, raise my thumb to signal, and mouth back "Uno." Within moments the peach-flavored, foam-topped concoction arrives. Harry, a man from Boston who managed this bar for the late Giuseppe Cipriani (of Hotel Cipriani fame), came up with this drink to refresh visitors who sought solace from the heavy heat of the Venetian summer. On this cold afternoon, its effect is just as delightful. The cocktail is a blend of white peach juice and prosecco (a sparkling Italian Champagne-like beverage). It is named after the fifteenth-century Venetian painter Giovanni Bellini—though no one seems to know why his name was chosen. I warm to the room and drink and begin to take in my fellow Bellini sippers.

The barman is as excited about mixing another drink as a man being led to the gallows. Sullen-faced and decidedly bored, he pours, mixes, blends, re-pours, and serves. A trio of drinkers lean against the bar, one barely sitting on a barstool. They laugh nervously at the topic of discussion, whatever that may be. Next to me an American couple sit in silence, slowly sipping their drinks, his a scotch on the rocks, hers a Bellini. They don't speak, not one word, the whole time they are in the bar. Next to them a large gathering of well-dressed, wealthy young people—wealthy in the sense of nouveau riche— Ferragamo-shoed, D&G-shirted, perfectly smooth and lovely—chatter on cell phones. A particular beauty takes a photo with her phone. To the delight of all at the table, she receives a picture from someone, da Parigi—*in Paris*. What a world.

The room has a haze to it. Steam from rain-soaked clothing mixes with the animated breath of conversation and the constant flash and whir of white-jacketed waiters. The second Bellini is taking its toll on me. Shadows of great artists linger here. Those whose writings, voices, paintings, or sculptures inspired generations all came here before it was fashionable with the current crowd. This is a clubby kind of establishment: subtle-colored walls, topped with old engravings of the city, surround a luminous dark bar with a sheen and patina only time can impart. A huge mirrored back bar adds to the feeling of being in the most conservative of such places, be they in New York, Sydney, or London.

A crash sounds through the bar. Our man drooping on the barstool has overturned a waiter's load of Bellinis. Mess and fuss ensue. Voices are raised as the offender slowly and unsteadily rises to his feet. He pulls out a platinum-colored credit card.

"The next round, for the house. On me," he says. Applause. All is forgiven.

Mops appear in the hands of the waiters. Soon, an unexpected fresh drink in hand, we all return to our various conversations and thoughts. The shadows of evening come early this time of year and, too soon, dark descends on the city.

The gorgeous young Italians have disappeared, I overhear, for dinner at the Danieli, another of Venice's posh haunts. The speechless American couple has left, as has the drink-buying trio from the bar. Peanuts and snacks arrive, an appetizer before dinner. I'm hopeful that the food will help fill the corners of a hungry stomach. The earlier commotion of the bar has settled down. A quieter, gentler, kind of timeless elegance takes its place. The barman is new, decidedly more interested in his work than his predecessor. A few more customers arrive—and all order a Bellini.

For more than seventy years, visitors have come to experience Harry's Bar. Perhaps some come to be seen. But most, I believe, come to share the same space known by so many creative talents over so many decades. That knowledge is shared through the medium of the delightful and smooth warming liquid known as the Bellini.

On the leisurely walk back to my hotel, I imagine an unknown Hemingway, alcohol-buzzed, slowly making his way home. Thousands of miles from family, many artists have, I am certain, left Harry's Bar and wandered the streets of late night Venice, totally enraptured by the city, completely oblivious to the day or the hour. Thanks to a certain Harry, I too discover that same sense of Venice. As I stroll Bellini-numbed through dark alleyways and piazzas, the city rises and steadies me as I find my way home.

Vendemmia

Early morning breezes at the villa now warn of coming winter. For the past few days, there has been increased activity in the vineyards. As I walk along the edge of the vines, Signora Bianca appears. She wears layers of clothing over her slight frame, good protection from the chill air of a late September morning. Her son and daughter-in-law are working along a line of vines and they bend to the labor of cutting the grape from the vines. Ten or so people are scattered throughout the vineyard. The grapes are ready. It is time. The vendemmia has started.

"Ah, you are ready!" She smiles at me. "I am glad that you asked to help with the harvest this year."

I pick up a large plastic basket. Giorgio, one of the

workmen, hands me a pair of sharp, curved cutters. We stand in front of grape-laden vines.

"Where do I cut the grapes?" I ask. He laughs.

His hand wraps around a cluster of deep red fruit and clips high up along the stem.

"Give the grapes some room," he says, more to the vine than to me.

I take my place alongside other workers and bend to the task at hand. Few words are exchanged. The clusters of grapes are collected in plastic containers. Once the containers are full, two of us lug them up, or down, the hill to a large cart. The cart will eventually carry the grapes up to the fattoria for the crush. There is little conversation. Signora Bianca approaches.

"It is wonderful to see you working with us."

"This is a great pleasure for me, Signora."

A stiff wind cuts through the rows of vines. I feel the chill even through my sweatshirt and jacket.

"We haven't much time, you know," she adds. "The frost arrives in two days and we have much to do." She circles her hand out around her. The hillsides all around us are full of grapes that are ready for the harvest.

"We take great pride in our wine."

The Sangiovese grape is a stunner to behold. Large deep magenta grapes, full, round, and ready for harvest hang beneath gold and green leaves. The vines have roots that reach nearly four feet into the rocky, dry soil. It is the plant's ability to reach minerals and water, particularly in the scorching, drought-prone heat of July and August, that sustains and fortifies the fruit.

As we work alongside each other, I think about the culture of this country. Here are the people of the village, octogenarians and the young alike, all gathered in the work of the land. They know that some of their group will not survive to enjoy the flavorful aged results of their work. They all know that someone, someday, will pour a glass of wine produced from the day that their hands touched the grape.

The sun moves steadily overhead. After a short break for a lunch of fresh cheese, sliced meats, water, and a single glass of local Chianti, we are back to the work. Some of the workers leave in midafternoon. By the time dark descends on our labor, only a few of us remain to cut the last remaining grapes from the far corner of the vineyard.

Signora Bianca and her daughter-in-law, Anna, take off their gloves and lean against the tires of a tractor. I walk up to join them. They are all smiles. Signora Bianca points upward as we all turn to watch a flock of birds heading south in the deepening blue of the sunset sky.

"So," she sighs. "What do you think?"

"I will have to ask my back and arms tomorrow."

We all laugh and walk up the muddy lane that connects this part of the vineyard to the villa. It has been a good day, full of honest labor and shared with people who are becoming friends.

A few weeks later I enjoy a glass of Chianti on the terrace. The bottle carries the label of nearby San Vito. The sun is low in the sky. There is no one else at the villa. A squirrel scurries by. A line of ants crawl across the stone edge of the terrace.

I sip the wine and think of the hands that struggled years ago to bring the grape to the factory. Hands that ensured the grape was crushed and placed in oak barrels. Hands of the vintners who tasted and worried over their wine, and of the Italians who love this land and all that it produces.

Winter will arrive soon. Our first frost came, as Signora Bianca had predicted, only two days after we completed the harvest. In the last rays of a russet-colored sunset I toast the

Italians and their appreciation for the abundance that surrounds every day of the life that they live.

Tables

Cooking Lesson

In the late afternoon, Signora Bianca arrives at the villa to prepare dinner. As the color of the sky begins to shift toward what I call evening-long light, I hear the rattle of fenders and the crunch of tires on the pine cone–strewn path that serves as a driveway. It's a good mile and a half from the village, and the signora accomplishes the trek on a bike purchased in 1972 when she was . . . well, she never has told me her age—however old she was, then.

Two evenings ago, I had approached her at the conclusion of dinner and asked if I might observe her prepare a meal. She'd smiled and made a characteristically Italian gesture, lifting her shoulders and making an easy wave of her right arm across the front of her body. It's body language for "Whatever you'd like." She has promised that she will prepare a dinner, in my presence, two days later.

The appointed day has arrived.

She greets me on the terrace with two large plastic sacks chock full of goods. I take them. She curls her finger temptingly and says that she is ready to "let me watch."

I follow her into the kitchen and help unpack the sacks. They contain two plump fresh chicken breasts from the butcher shop in town ("Fresh today," she says); six fresh brown eggs; four deep red tomatoes that she places on the windowsill; an onion; some fresh salt and pepper, each carefully wrapped in wax paper that has been folded in the shape of an envelope; a batch of fresh asparagus; one large clove of garlic; and a large bottle of olive oil, extra virgin ("We needed some more," she quips).

She pulls a sprig of fresh basil from the pocket of her apron and sets it on the counter. Out comes a large wooden cutting board. I begin to unwrap the asparagus.

"Over there," she says sternly. "You watch. *I* cook!" She turns her attention to the task at hand. "Go get two sprigs of rosemary."

I obediently head out of the kitchen and onto the terrace. From one of huge bushes that stand on either side of the terrace, I pull two large twigs and return, triumphant, to the kitchen.

"Alora," I say. *Here you go.* "Rosmarino."

The signora points to the counter to the right of the stove. "There, please," she says.

She pours a liberal amount of olive oil into a large black skillet. A blue flame wraps around the edge from underneath the pan. She opens the door to the oven and makes certain it is on. After carefully opening the wax paper envelopes, she pinches salt and pepper into the skillet. She takes up the wide blade of her cooking knife and slams it flat against the garlic clove, then deftly slices the garlic in two. Half of the clove goes into the skillet, along with two chicken breasts. She motions me out of the way.

As she picks up a bottle of the local Chianti wine she says, "Open this, please."

I uncork the bottle and place it next to the stove. She pours about a cup of the deep red liquid into the skillet. Everything in the skillet sizzles as the wine deglazes the simmering mixture. A plume of smoke rises into the kitchen. It smells like heaven. She gets a glass from the cabinet and pours some of the Chianti into it, recorks the bottle, and takes a deep gulp.

"Ah," she sighs. "Like the sun."

Out comes another, smaller skillet. She again baptizes it with olive oil and some salt and pepper, then adds the other half of the garlic clove. She turns the chicken breast. Again, a cloud of aromatic steam fills the kitchen. The eggs are cracked and poured into a large ceramic mixing bowl, now empty of its usual cargo of fruit. She whisks the eggs with a fork and sets them aside.

"Later," she mumbles.

The asparagus meets the cutting board and knife as she skillfully slices it into half-inch pieces. They go into a small pot of boiling water. She pulls the skillet with the chicken off of the flame and then carefully places it into the heated oven.

"You wait," she says to the birds. The chicken breasts disappear behind the white enameled door of the stove.

The fresh tomatoes that she has placed on the windowsill fall prey to the knife. In a matter of seconds they are sliced and spread across a ceramic platter. The asparagus is drained in the sink. She sets it aside.

She then removes two large balls of mozzarella cheese from a plastic bag, slices them, and places the bright cloud-white pieces on top of the tomatoes. The sprig of basil is stripped of its leaves. She scatters the pieces of leaves across the platter. Fresh olive oil and balsamic vinegar are drizzled over the salad. Salt and pepper are gingerly sprinkled over the dish. The salad is prepared in a matter of three minutes, and it looks straight out of a wonderful Tuscan cookbook.

She directs her attention back to the ceramic bowl. The asparagus and eggs are mixed together. She uses a hand-held shredder to flake fresh Parmigiano-Reggiano cheese into the mixture, then pours it all into the skillet. It, too, sizzles, and soon the "frittata di asparagi" is turned over in the pan.

I am dispatched to the terrace with linens, tableware, plates and glasses. Table set, I walk back into the front room of the villa. The fragrances filling the house make my mouth water and my appetite soar. When I return to the kitchen, the frittata is done and rests on a small tray. Bits of rosemary cover the chicken.

"The salad," she says, "can go."

She points to the door. I obey. She follows me with the frittata in one hand and the chicken dish in the other. She places it on the table and turns to go.

"Thank you, Signora Bianca."

She smiles, shrugs that inimitably Italian shrug and says, "So now, you have seen me cook. I don't understand." She shakes her head.

"What?" I ask.

She touches together the fingers of her left hand. It looks like one of those shadow puppets I used to make as a kid.

"I don't understand why you Americans are so interested in our cooking. It's all so simple."

She wipes her hands on the apron. I watch her walk back to the main door of the house. Signora Bianca is somewhat bow-legged and the slippers on her feet list to the outside.

She disappears into the shadows. I now understand why so many Americans love Italian food; the answer lies at the heart of preparing these meals.

As I bite into luscious red tomatoes and sup on fresh asparagus frittata and roasted chicken, I recall the words that capture why this food is incredibly good: "It's all so simple."

May in Chianti

ncient grapevines silhouette against the horizon, their limbs reaching into smoke and haze. Around a tight curve a medieval church appears in a hillside corner. Its damp hand-hewn stones sparkle against the bright May light. Red poppies appear amid tall green grasses beneath groves of olive trees. The sky above the mist is brilliant azure blue. The hillsides of Tuscany awaken to a promising May morning.

The S2 highway winds from Florence to Siena. The roadway traces the road upon which Romans, marching armies, and travelers have for centuries found their way. The Caesars of Rome, the warring popes, and armies of the Second World War have marched along this road. What now draws people to this part of Italy, this heart of the Chianti region, are grapes, primarily the Sangiovese, and the incredible wines that are produced by private wineries along the Chianti road. Between Montevarchi and Greve in Chianti there are no fewer than fifteen small, mostly family-owned, wineries. I am looking forward to meeting some friends who are staying at a villa outside of Montevarchi, forty-five minutes south of Florence.

Clara, an Englishwoman who used to work in Rome, found her villa more than forty years ago. She has carefully and tenderly revitalized the land around it. The harvest of luscious grapes and olives increases with each passing year. Bea and Edith, friends from my first season in Italy, are visiting Clara for a few weeks. We are to meet at the villa and then drive to Il Cenacolo, an excellent restaurant near Cavriglia, about thirty minutes from her villa.

Several gorgeous homes stand near the gravel road that leads up to the "Little Hill," Clara's villa. One house is a deep ochre color with bright blue shutters. Another, perched on a nearby hill, glistens with bright orange stucco, its driveway lined with tall, verdant Italian cypresses. A farmyard near the road is full of chickens. Dogs race wildly around the yard. The day's laundry hangs in the hot afternoon sun. A woman waves as we pass by.

Clara is waiting on her small front porch. She stands and waves. Bea appears from inside the villa; greetings abound. The news of the day is exchanged as Bea and I wend our way around the house to the back. Edith is resting in the shade of an old oak tree, a book open on her lap. Reunions of this kind, so far from home, seem more intense, more urgent. We talk of the weather, of Edith's upcoming art show in New York City and of Art Workshop International, the company that Bea and Edith have owned for over twenty years. After a few hours we gather our things and drive to the restaurant.

Il Cenacolo was opened in the 1980s by a family that

can trace its lineage to the fifteenth century. Lush green ivy covers the entire front wall of the restaurant. It is a gorgeous day. The restaurant is empty and the owner's wife explains that we really didn't need a reservation. "It is too early in the season," she says.

The menus are presented. We consider some of the offerings, all excellent: chicken livers prepared in an orange sauce; fresh pasta stuffed with porcini mushrooms and truffles; fava bean soup; freshly grilled duck, placed in small ravioli with cheese topping; vegetables, from the owner's garden, prepared on the grill with olive oil, salt, and pepper. The wine list is more spectacular than the food. More than fifty different labels are offered, primarily Chiantis from this area of Tuscany. The waiter recommends a bottle. We order.

A warm breeze flows into the room from an open window near our table. Wine and glasses arrive. Clara has been coming to small restaurants in this region for many years, and she talks about the changes that she has seen.

"When I first discovered the villa, a real rat of a place, I was only thirty-eight and felt lucky to have found it for such a great price." She sips from her glass, and smiles.

"I must say that my wine is equally as good as this, don't you think?" She looks at Bea, whose hands are folded on the table as she listens.

"Clara, you have the best of everything—a villa, wonderful wines and olive oil—truly a good life."

Edith stares out the window, lost in some thought.

"Well," Clara continues, "it has been, and is, a good life. Now that I no longer have to work in Rome, I can spend much more time here. I do love it so."

The waiter brings the first course, some small ravioli covered in thin, light, flakes of fresh truffle. He drizzles a bit of golden-colored olive oil over the pasta. The flavors are rich yet not heavy, complemented by the texture of fresh pasta. We grow silent as the food slowly disappears from our plates. The waiter returns with our main course. I enjoy grilled pork with steamed fresh vegetables. Bea and Edith trade portions of Florentine steak and grilled chicken, both presented with small, crisp, cubed potatoes that have been prepared in olive oil. The plates are steaming hot when they arrive. We fall into a nearly reverential silence as the plates are cleaned of their flavorful bounty.

We have been the only diners in the restaurant throughout the meal and have enjoyed particularly attentive service. The waiter returns to tempt us with luscious desserts: a dried fruit cake, dark chocolate cake served with fresh raspberry sauce, or a small assortment of chocolates from Slitti, a famous Tuscan chocolate shop. We look at each other and ponder the choices. We opt just for coffee.

"May we have our coffee out on the terrace?" Clara asks the waiter.

"Yes, of course." The waiter nods towards the door. "We will bring it to you."

We find a simple wooden table in the shade of a wisteria-covered arbor. Coffee is served. Sunlight filters through leaves and branches. Bees hum and buzz around the nearby roses. The scent of wisteria mixes with the sweet odor of the roses. A sparrow, searching for a handout, hops near the table as a large dog lazes in the full sun on the graveled driveway.

We sit for another hour to talk, beneficiaries of a particularly quiet day at the restaurant. It is a bright, sun-filled afternoon. A gathering of friends satiated by fresh Tuscan food is but one of the many gifts of this fascinating land. For now it is enough to breathe deeply the verdant bounty of Tuscany surrounding us, and to dream of a day when we too might call this place home.

Bibe

Five generations of the Baudone family have honed a tradition of excellent dining at the Trattoria Bibe. Annusca, the daughter of the current owners, learned the craft of simple and flavorful Tuscan cooking from her mother, Liliana. Her brothers, Andrea and Fabio, take care of the guests with poise and natural ease.

I first met the Baudone family when I visited their Trattoria during my first season in Florence. Located in the small town of Galluzzo, only a mile and a half from the center of Florence, the Trattoria stands along a busy street. What was once a narrow gravel road used by carts and horses is now a paved road where cars whisk by at breathtaking speed. In 1937 the famous Italian poet Eugenio Montale wrote *Bibe a Ponte All'Asse,* a work of praise for the food and service. A collection of paintings and drawings by Tuscan artists covers the interior walls of the building. The walkway from the car park passes through a large garden. As I approach the main entrance, the youngest son, Fabio, greets me. Within minutes he introduces me to his "Papa" behind the bar in the foyer and ushers me into the kitchen.

Liliana Scarselli Baudone, the mother of the current generation managing the restaurant, is a warm, engaging woman. Her silver hair, pin-neat dress and apron, and ready smile immediately set visitors at ease. She has a wide and open face that invites conversation. We talk for a few moments, and then she introduces me to another member of the family, Annusca, who is hard at work on the opposite side of a huge kitchen table.

Annusca is a tall woman with large brown eyes, a round face, and a warm, easy smile. Her gray-streaked hair is pulled back tightly, secured by a red ribbon. Sweat glistens on her forehead. I thank her for the opportunity to visit the kitchen. She continues to talk with the other members of the kitchen staff, tending to the food, as she shakes my hand.

"A dopo," she says.

I excuse myself from the kitchen. Andrea, the eldest of the three children, hands me a menu at a garden terrace table.

The great tradition of the Tuscan kitchen, and of a family's dedication to an extraordinary experience, is evident on every page of the menu. It is uncomplicated, yet every dish entices with the promise of spices, olive oil, and careful preparation. Andrea shares the specialties that Annusca has prepared. For the antipasti, first a crostini con caponata di verdure (a simple crust of bread, browned and served with fresh vegetables). She also is offering fiori di zucca farciti di ricotta e zucchine fritti (zucchini flowers filled with ricotta cheese, lightly breaded and then fried in olive oil).

For the first course the special of the evening is pomodori gratinati aglio e prezzemolo (warm Roma tomatoes, served with grated basil and oregano, grated cheese and garlic). Annusca offers, for the second course, a crespelle ai fungi porcini (porcini mushrooms served inside a small crepe, heated with fresh cheese), or a lasagne con zucchine and taleggio (fresh, free-form lasagna, created with zucchini and the day's fresh, thin, delicate wide pasta noodles). By the time Andrea is through reviewing this incredible selection of foods I wonder how Annusca is able to create such meals in that small, busy kitchen.

As I make my selections, Andrea's smile encourages my choice. A bottle of Chianti is ordered. He leaves me to the quiet of an early evening. The sun reddens the sky. Clouds slowly float overhead as evening light paints them orange, red, and purple. An occasional car flashes by on the road. Ivy covers the facade of the Trattoria. Planters overflow with geraniums, rosemary, and lavender. The entrance is illuminated by a small warm lamp set on a dark wood bar. As Andrea returns with the bottle of wine, I ask him about this place, about how it came to be.

He checks to make sure that all of the occupied tables are taken care of and then takes a seat. "My great-grandfather started this Trattoria when the road here"—he points to the nearby fence—"was only a gravel cart path. Travelers on the way south to Siena or the hill towns outside of Florence would often stop and ask for refreshment sometimes a place to stay and so it was that Trattoria Bibe was born."

"Where does the name 'Bibe' come from?"

"Tradition has it that it was my great-grandmother's nickname, one of affection and love." He stares down at my glass of Chianti and smiles one of those distant, remembering smiles. Evening darkness has fallen on us.

"Thank you."

"My pleasure. I should get back to work." He smiles. "We have a restaurant to run, you know."

Candles flicker on the table. Dinner comes and goes far too quickly and, finally, Fabio reappears to ask if I would like any dessert. As tempting as that sounds, I thank him and decline. This meal has been bountiful, and will carry memories with it even as months pass.

But a further surprise—even more delightful than the desserts I have just declined—is in store. Fabio returns with news that Annusca has invited me back to the kitchen for a brief visit. I settle my bill quickly, eager to talk with the Baudone women as they work.

Annusca's Kitchen

White-jacketed cooks move with purpose in the rear of the kitchen. Annusca, standing behind a long metal-topped work table, is focused on final preparations for several dishes. On the other side of the table, comfortably seated in a high wooden-backed stool, is Signora Baudone. Her silent observations of the work and gentle smile betray a certain reverence for the activity in the kitchen. Signora Baudone stands as I enter and gives me a strong handshake.

I thank them both for an incredible meal.

Annusca puts the final touches on four steaming and bubbling servings of hot pasta, smothered in light, frothy cheese. Signora Baudone takes her seat again and ever so quietly begins to watch Annusca at work.

"It has always been like this," she says. "My mother once sat where I am now, and I used to work on the other side of this same table." She softly taps its surface. "Her mother before her did the same thing. It is how we continue our tradition of serving fresh, flavorful food."

One of the waiters takes the plates of pasta, even as another brings in a new order. Annusca continues cooking as her mother sits, arms crossed, watching the meals come and go.

The next dish Annusca prepares is a chocolate dessert. She swirls hot dark chocolate over a small chocolate cake and then sprinkles the tiniest bit of cinnamon over it all. One of the kitchen staff brings her a container of fresh homemade vanilla gelato (ice cream). Just as the waitress enters to carry it out to a customer, Annusca garnishes the cake with a frozen ball of ice cream.

I stand in the corner of the kitchen and watch as dish after dish of food is prepared in a nearly unending parade. Entrees alternate with soups, desserts, beefsteak Florentine, fresh hot porcini mushrooms, battered and fried, stuffed zucchini blossoms—more and more until there are just too many to count or remember. Annusca meets all of the demands with aplomb and grace.

Signora Baudone rises from her chair, takes my arm, and gently leads me out of the kitchen. There is a labyrinth of dining rooms and hallways inside the Trattoria. She guides me to a wall that is covered with sketches and photographs of family and points to a particular portrait.

"My grandfather and grandmother—the Bibe. And there," she adds, touching a golden framed photograph, "are my parents."

I look over at her. A wistful melancholy passes over her face, and she nods.

"So long ago." Her voice trails off. She leads me into another room, where several pieces of art depicting the Trattoria are displayed. "This one was painted when my grandfather had just opened the business. It was done after a snowfall, and I think it is so beautiful." The signora releases my arm and gently settles in a nearby chair. She motions to a chair nearby for me.

"I remember playing in the garden behind the Trattoria as a child. There are days now, as I pass on our traditions to my daughter and grandson, that I can't believe the time has gone by so fast."

One of the waitresses interrupts to ask her about an order, a problem with payment. The signora asks her to talk with Fabio. The waitress turns and is gone.

"I am so proud of all that our family has accomplished. Our roots are here, and even though I have never traveled far, the world has come to us."

She pauses for a few moments to take a deep breath, then lets out a long sigh. "So many friends from around the world come here so many times. As it is with you, Marco. You have been here many times."

She places her hand on mine. "For people who understand what we do and why we do it, as you do, it is not work. It is our pleasure."

Fabio appears in the door of the room and says something that I don't understand. The signora rises from her chair.

"So," she breathes, "I must go back to the kitchen."

As we stand together I look, again, at the painting of the Trattoria, completed those many years ago.

"Thank you for all that you have done to make Italy come alive for so many," I say to her.

She smiles and disappears around the corner of the hallway.

I walk down the garden path to the car. A cat follows me with some sure hope of a treat. The parking lot is nearly empty. Silver shadows, cast from the moon's light, dot the gravel. A slight breeze shakes the leaves above me. The air is filled with the light scent of food from the kitchen. Quiet conversation floats up from behind the garden wall. One of the voices I recognize as that of Annusca.

As I drive the narrow road back toward Florence, it comes to me that what this wonderful family does with their hands, what the past generations accomplished, was summed up in something that Signora Baudone said. *It is not our work. It is our pleasure.*

It must be true across Italy that, for generations, families have prepared flavorful meals built on that simple statement. When friends gather around a table to eat, such meals not only sustain us, they give us pleasure and feed our memories. The spirit of ancestors gathers at table as well. Each recipe prepared reminds us where we came from, that time goes too fast, and we should take pleasure in every savory bite.

Dorando

owers in the medieval hill town of San Gimignano have reached into the Tuscan sky for more than seven centuries. Once the possession of wealthy families, the towers have seen much change along the historic route between Florence and Siena. In the Middle Ages the town was a principal site on the Via Francigena, the pilgrimage route between Canterbury, in England, and Rome. Today, throngs of tourists come to enjoy the beauty of a stunningly preserved village. I look forward to a visit to one of my favorite restaurants in the whole of Italy, a place where the importance of food in the Italian culture becomes clear.

The main street of the village leads to the Piazza Cisterna, so named for the well in the center of the square. Visitors lounge in the umbrella shade of cafés, enjoying quiet conversation. Piazza Duomo, the large open space that fronts the Collegiata Church, is only a few steps beyond the well. A clutch of tourists sit on the precipitous stairs that front the church. Others wander in and out of the handful of shops that entice the curious with photographs of Italy, artwork by local artisans, or ceramics made in the nearby hills. Just beyond the square is a narrow alley. A small sign on the wall reads "Dorando: Slow Food." I walk quickly past the crowds that loiter near the almost indistinguishable alleyway and find myself at the entrance to the restaurant.

A tiny space just off of the passageway leads to the entrance. Dorando is an unimposing place. Etched glass doors welcome diners to three vaulted rooms, all covered in white stucco. The owner greets me at the door. I take a seat in the back corner of the restaurant. There are no views here. Rather, the owner's family places emphasis on the quality of the food, the experience of decanting good wines, and attentive service.

The menu arrives. It never ceases to amaze with its variety and quality. To start, I consider leek and herb tartlets with sautéed chopped mushrooms or a slice of smoked duck and sautéed broccoli presented with a walnut pesto sauce. For the first course, among many offerings, is risotto with asparagus tops, sliced scallops in a shrimp bisque, and tagliatelle (large hand-made pasta) with sausages, small onion, dried tomatoes, and smoked ricotta flakes. For a second course, they offer roast guinea hen, suckling pig simmered in the oven, or grilled beef loin . . . the choices are too many and too wonderful to imagine. I review the wine menu and select a little-known Chianti from the Classico region of Tuscany.

The "slow food" movement was started in Italy to counteract changes made to the dining experience by fast-food restaurants. The owners of cafés and restaurants that follow the slow food movement pride themselves on fresh food and the time that it takes to prepare. In all of the times that I have enjoyed a meal here, there never has been any hurry or any sense that diners must move quickly through a meal—the very reason that reservations are required.

The owner's wife explains that she will decant the wine and let it breathe for about twenty minutes before serving it with the appetizer. Slow food, indeed. She places a large crystal decanter on a side cart that has been rolled up next to the table. After presenting the wine, she methodically uncovers and uncorks the bottle. She sniffs the cork and places it next to me on the table. A long glass rod is placed into the decanter. She takes the tip of the open wine bottle and gently lays it against the glass pole. The wine moves delicately out of the bottle and begins to twist itself around the glass, eventually finding its way to the bottom of the decanter. As the wine slowly spirals down into the carafe I think of grapes in the sun, the years that the wine has aged in French oak casks and the vintner's discriminating palate . . . all for this moment. The last drop of wine traces the curve of the glass and rests in the decanter. She sets the empty bottle upright on the side table, smiles, and walks away.

A large bottle of Pellegrino water arrives, along with a mouth-watering selection of oven-fresh breads. Other diners enter and are seated. The music of Gregorian chant drifts out from small speakers placed discreetly throughout the restaurant. In what seems a very short time, my appetizer arrives. The wine is poured, and the tastes of true Tuscan food are all that fill the next hour and a half.

Food: Italians are passionate about preparing it, serving it, enjoying it. They are sustained by the bounty of the earth, and they know well the produce of the seasons. Around any Italian table there is often animated discussion about wine, vineyards, mushrooms, pasta, and vegetables, and the way these have been served. A direct connection exists in the Italian culture between sea, land, and life. It is nowhere more evident than in the kitchens, cafés, and restaurants of this ever-fascinating country.

Teatro del Sale

Theater of Knows Them? Theater in the Room? I go to the Italian dictionary, a thick, well-worn tome that has become a close friend, and settle on "theater in the round." Round as in circle. Circle as in all-encompassing. Teatro del Sale is a wonderful place where people gather, where food meets passion, and where art and music blend.

It is a rainy evening in late May. I'm standing across the street from a famous Florentine restaurant, Cibreo. The area around the San Ambrogio market is full of activity. Visitors stomp by. Conversations in English, Japanese, Italian, and German fade past me under the protective cover near the entrance of the restaurant-cum-performance venue.

Friends arrive. One, a now famous Tuscan playwright, Angelo Salveli, is wrapped in dark tweed, scarf, and corduroys. The other, Giancarlo Mordini, manages and directs the Rifredi Theater, a center of performance art recognized for bold and imaginative productions. He is all blue tonight in jeans, turtleneck, and jacket. We shake hands and enter.

Thick, etched-glass art deco doors swing open to reveal a warm wood-paneled room. Giancarlo explains that Fabio Picchi and his wife, Maria Cassi, restored this ancient convent only a few years ago.

Fabio has a presence. Silver hair frames a true Tuscan face. Bright blue eyes flash as he comes from behind the bar to greet us. Heads turn in the room as he moves. This is the capo, the boss. Angelo immediately engages Fabio in conversation. Maria, a bundle of energy and enthusiasm, immediately engages Giancarlo in discussion. They pull ahead, laughing as they walk into a large, timber-framed room.

Worn, oversized leather chairs have been pulled together so that small groups of friends can talk. The aromas of garlic, rosemary, roasting meats, and bread fill the air. To our right is a group of people who have gathered around a very long wooden table full of steaming dishes. Behind the table are several huge windows that allow us to see into the kitchen. It is there, in the kitchens of the teatro, that magic is made.

The kitchen is at one end of the room; a stage with rich blue velvet curtains frames the back wall. All around us are straight-backed chairs, pulled into haphazard groupings. Groups of friends whisper across plates of steaming fresh food. Giancarlo signals for me to move close to the stage. Two wooden chairs and two ebony music stands rest, empty, on the left side of the stage. I leave my jacket on our chosen three chairs and move around and through the crowd toward the food table.

The food is served buffet style. Serving dishes fill every inch of the tabletop. Someone slides open one of the kitchen windows and loudly announces to the room, "Asparagi con olio e parmigiano!" (Asparagus in olive oil with Parmesan cheese). Heads turn as a waitress rushes up to the cook. The fresh food replaces an empty casserole on the table. Dark, verdant spears of asparagus are bathed in olive oil. Fresh shaved Parmesan cheese delicately covers the platter. I lunge for a large spoon and place a few pieces on my plate.

"The kitchen is run by Fabio," Giancarlo explains. "He has one of the best Tuscan kitchens—if not *the* best—across the street at Cibreo. "This place was designed so that there would be at least one place where Florentines could gather to share a love of theater and great food. During the day members of the 'teatro' can rest, read, study, or relax. They offer breakfast, lunch, and dinner, all buffet style.

"Now, let me explain the food." Giancarlo uses his fork to point at various servings of food as he describes them. The first dish, tortellini con spinaci e formaggio, is tiny pasta envelopes, stuffed with ground spices, blended with finely chopped spinach, topped by chopped tomato. The tortellini are piled high on the plate, though a number have already disappeared.

"This is chicken, fresh from the rotisserie," Giancarlo continues. Browned breasts of chicken sizzle on a hot griddle. Rosemary dots the meat. I take one. "And this," Giancarlo says, pointing to a large flat bowl of fettuccine laced with bright red chunks of tomato, garlic, olive oil, and pepper, "is fettuccine con pomodori, aglio, e pepe."

My mouth is awash. I can barely take this all in. Cut green beans await our palates nearby. A thick brew of fagioli, wonderful Italian beans (a staple of Florentine and Tuscan cooking) fill a large brown bowl.

Across the table is a pan with potato gnocchi in tomato sauce. The tiny, luminous delicacies shimmer in the sauce. Giancarlo points out another treat: sliced, grilled green and sweet red peppers. They glisten in a coating of olive oil. By the time Giancarlo's gustatory tour is done, my plate is almost too heavy to lift. Such food!

We weave our way back to our seats. Delicious food that once filled our plates, and eyes now fills our stomachs. The air around us is still thick with scents of garlic, rosemary, perfume, cologne, and dark, rich coffee. To complete the meal, Giancarlo shows me a table with desserts: tiramisu, dark thick chocolate cake, and fresh whipped cream stand ready to be consumed. We don't hesitate.

Fabio, the owner, suggests we move to the back of the room, where there are more comfortable seats. "You will be able to see better."

The level of noise in the room settles to a gentle hum. The lights dim in the room as Fabio appears in front of the stage. He says that we will hear music performed by a guitarist and a violinist whom he first heard in Bologna. His calm, peaceful manner is mesmerizing. The room is now silent. Lights in the kitchen are turned off.

The two musicians appear on stage. They place their sheet music on the shiny stands. Windows in the darkened kitchen silently open to the room. The staff, including the chef, lean out onto the sills to listen.

The violinist's round face is punctuated by brilliant round brown eyes. As he plays, his eyebrows arch. His eyes close. He seems to lose himself into the notes, pining for the beauty that the instrument makes. The guitar player has a noble nose and a long, dark ponytail. His lower jaw protrudes in a way that reminds me of the face of Cosimo de Medici, the founder of the great banking empire that eventually ensured this city's artistic heritage. Occasionally the guitarist nods at certain points in the music. Music of Vivaldi and Granados, flamenco, lyrical strains of Brazilian music, even a few tunes of Paul McCartney ("Michelle") and

Pink Floyd, rewritten to accommodate these instruments, fills the space. Strong and vital applause follow the conclusion of each piece.

During the concert I look over toward the kitchen. Candlelight gleams from atop the now empty food table. Faces of the kitchen staff flicker in and out of golden light as the flame reacts to the slight current of air in the room. Their shadows dance, nearly in time to the music, against the stucco wall behind them. To my left a young woman takes the hand of the man next to her. Their fingers intertwine and hold on. Rain taps against large panels of glass high over our heads. Music weaves through the room, around columns that once heard the music of the church.

The final piece of music is a long, slow, sensual piece by the Baroque period composer Arcangelo Corelli. As the performance concludes, the musicians stand to accept the enthusiastic applause. How wonderful it would be if the echoes of their music could float out of this place, spill into the streets of Florence, and we could return to less complicated times. The city's history infuses us on evenings like this. Time seems to step back across centuries as ancient notes breathe new inspiration into our souls.

Our evening draws far too quickly to a close. Fabio and Maria spend time speaking with us about the next upcoming event. Maria, an accomplished dramatist, will perform. Promises are made to return. The teatro empties. We are the last to leave.

The rain has stopped as we make our way toward the Piazza della Repubblica, a huge open square in the heart of Florence. Lights from old palazzo windows are reflected on the rain-soaked cobblestones. We talk of the evening, of appreciation for such a place, such food, and such music. When it comes time to say good-bye, I find it nearly impossible to go. We shake hands. I watch the pair slowly disappear into the darkened distance. I find myself wishing for just one more evening in a theater where friends, food, and passionate appreciation for art and music join together.

Home Hearth

Luca della Robbia (1400–1482) was a Renaissance Florentine sculptor known for his fine work in clay. He was commissioned by Piero de Medici, founder of what was at the time the largest banking empire in the world, to create twelve large ceramic roundels to decorate the ceiling of a study in the Palazzo Medici in Florence. In the wake of wars and cultural change, the roundels have since been removed from the Medici palace and now form part of the collection at the Victoria and Albert Museum in London.

Each piece was to depict both the sign of the Zodiac and the main agricultural activity during the associated month. The roundel for November depicts a man harvesting olives. He uses a ladder to work, carefully gathering the fruit from the trees in the grove. In Tuscany to this day, olives are harvested in the same manner.

Janet Shapiro came to Tuscany from San Francisco in 1972, determined to build a new life for herself in Italy. She met and married Stefano Magazzini shortly after renting a small farmhouse in the hills south of Florence. Over the past thirty years the couple have raised two daughters, and between "real" work and family responsibilities have acquired more than three thousand olive trees. Their combined passion for producing the finest possible olive oil inspired them to create a business that now turns out some of the best oils made in Italy.

I first met Janet and Stefano several years ago, and it is in the course of a dinner at their home that I learn more about their work. Janet is standing next to the kitchen table in their cozy home. Stefano, whose passion for Tuscan cooking is rivaled only by his passion for the olive business, is slicing plump porcini mushrooms in preparation for the evening meal. His work table is covered with fresh lettuce, mushrooms, thick red beefsteaks, and fresh bread dough. Red and orange light from a fire in their raised hearth flashes into the room. Shadow, a six-month-old kitten, is curled up on a cushion while Lampone, their twelve-year-old dog, sits awaiting a possible treat.

"How did you come to name your company Sagittario?" I ask.

"We decided on the name," she explains, "from the sign of the Zodiac. Della Robbia's work for the month of harvest depicts a man up in the olive trees. We selected that roundel as the symbol for our company. November carries the sign of Sagittarius."

Stefano adds, in his deeply accented Tuscan English, "The art on the lunette is of a man climbing into a tree using a ladder. That is precisely how we go about harvesting the olives each year in our groves." As he talks, he uses an old wooden spoon as an extension of his hands, moving in a slow ballet as he further explains the art of making olive oil.

Janet smiles and points to the porcini mushrooms. Stefano smiles and returns to his preparation and cooking. Lampone suddenly muffles a bark, and the cat lifts her head from the pillow. There is movement outside the entryway door.

"Oh, it must be Carla," Janet says. "I cannot wait for you to meet her."

The door slowly opens and a lovely bright-faced woman enters the room. "I'm so sorry to intrude," she says, though no one imagines she is intruding in the least. Carla Geri has a dazzling wide smile and dark brown eyes. Silver-streaked hair surrounds a noble face, one etched with years of living from, and on, the land. She extends her hand. Lampone and the cat go back to their various slumbers.

"Carla has written over twenty-five cookbooks, you know?" Stefano says over his shoulder. He is leaning over the stove top, stirring fresh red peppers while keeping an eye on the frying, batter-dipped mushrooms. The room smells of earth and fire. There is a sparkle to the air, scented by peppers and the sweet deep perfume of the mushrooms.

The cookbook author gives a demure grin and shrugs her shoulders. "Well, I love to cook and my books are all about cooking, the art of Tuscan food and our recipes. My latest book is about the food of the court of the Medici. A friend shared with me a compilation of art, all about food, that the Medici family collected. The works have been stored for many years. We used full-color photographs of that art in the book. It has been well received."

Janet has poured a glass of Chianti wine for the signora, and I assist her to a chair next to the kitchen table. As she sits, the cat takes a long, vibrating stretch on her pillow. The fire crackles behind her.

"The fire feels wonderful," Carla says, "especially with the weather turning so cold. It is getting dark so early."

Janet explains, "Carla has been a close friend since I first found this house. She lives in a villa up the hill from us and loves to come by in the evening to see how we are doing. She is a very dear friend."

"Salute!" She raises her glass of wine to us all. *To your good health.*

"This wine," Janet says, "comes from a very special friend's family who lives in the Chianti area of Tuscany, south of Florence. Stefano believes, as I do, that it is among the best."

Stefano takes a few items off of the stove and sets them away from the fire on the work table. "Mark," he says, "come with me. I will show you the forno, my hand-built, wood-burning oven." He reaches over to a bowl in which wonderful thick dough has been rising. A large handful of raisins is tossed into the bowl. He works the ingredients together with his hands.

"Come." He takes the bowl and leads me up the narrow, curving stairs to the back door of their home. As we leave, Signora Geri calls out, "Be careful with that fire, Stefano!"

"Of course," he says. We walk into the garden. The forno is made of brick and has an arched opening above a hinged iron door. Smoke slowly rises from the chimney. Stefano says that he made it in one summer with the help of a friend. He takes a stick and opens the door to the fire. Deep red embers glow in the dark recesses of the oven. He gathers a few branches of drying oak from a nearby stack of wood, breaking some of the branches into smaller pieces and placing a few of the shorter branches in the fire. He presses the dough mixture flat onto a round metal disk and, using his fingers, creates a wavy surface on the dough.

"Schiacciata is my favorite bread," Stefano tells me. "Since I was a child, this bread has sustained me and the family. You can use the basic dough with raisins, grapes, or sweets or with just rosemary and olive oil." As he talks, the round disk is placed into the oven, a short distance from the heated embers. "There—it will rest until it is ready."

Janet appears from around the corner of the house. "Carla is just leaving if you would like to say good-bye," she says.

"Yes, of course, Mark, you go ahead. I will be back inside in a few minutes."

Signora Geri is standing in the kitchen, hand extended, as I reenter the room. As she shakes my hand she says, "It was a pleasure to meet you." She smiles. "Ciao, Janet. A dopo." She opens the door and is quickly gone.

Moments later, Stefano appears. Steam rises from the bread. He places the platter of bread on the work table, picks up a knife, and cuts several pie-shaped pieces for us. I taste. It is extraordinary—light, full of the sweetness from the raisins. It is amazing, and I tell them so.

"I am so pleased that you enjoy it," Stefano says. From out of the oven he pulls a large copper pot full of pork ribs bubbling in their own juices. A small flat pan full of red and yellow peppers appears as well. The air is scented with rosemary, the bread, the peppers, and the meat. Lampone jumps to his feet, tail wagging. He saunters over to the door of the stove.

Stefano puts out his hand. "No, Lampone. Not now."

The pot finds its way onto the work table. Servings of the ribs are placed on plates for each of us. The battered and fried porcini mushrooms, and olive-oil-drenched red peppers, are passed around as well. Dinner is served. Lampone struggles for attention from under the table while we enjoy a delectable feast.

"Don't feed him," Janet says. "We discourage him, especially at his age."

What a meal. The food disappears as we share stories of our love for Tuscany, for Italian food and wine. Shadow, the cat, curls up on my lap and sleeps. The fire crackles and dwindles in the fireplace. Dishes are taken off the table and stacked in the sink. I offer to help but my hosts refuse, always returning to the table to talk further.

"You must come to visit our laboratorio where the olive oil is bottled and stored," Stefano says.

"With pleasure."

The evening concludes with thanks for the delicious meal and a promise to visit their laboratorio when time allows. The dog, Lampone, barks into the cool night air as I wave a good-bye and drive down the narrow, twisting road that passes by their house.

The days that Janet and Stefano spend in the olive groves, tending trees, take time and are far from easy. Generosity and kindness, a deep-seated and sincere honesty, surround this family. A warm hearth in their small hillside home is all they need or desire. Italians are attracted to style, fashion, and technology, as most of us are. What they care for more deeply are uncomplicated values, love of the land, and of family connections. I turn onto the main highway and head back to my "home," good fortune and gratitude my constant companions.

Hands

Emerald Rain

Olive trees line the gravel road that leads up to Janet and Stefano's workshop. Leaves flash silver and iridescent green in the morning light. Ladders lean into the trees. Workers tend to the olives. The narrow road that rises above the valley near Florence is steep and full of blind curves. I pull my car into a small meadow.

There is activity everywhere. The fruit of the harvest is, literally, raked from the branches. Olives fall from the trees like emerald rainfall, onto large nets laid around the bases of the trees. Workers move ladders from tree to tree. Small groups gather the olives and place them into plastic crates placed throughout the area. Quiet conversation fills the air.

The workshop is located in a borgo, a small community that once was home to two landowners and the tenant farmers' homes. Two chapels occupy opposite sides of a very small parking area. The keystone of the arch above the doorway to Janet and Stefano's workshop is dated 1635.

"This was originally a stable for this borgo," Janet says as we enter the building. Light enters the interior from a high window. Deep red terra-cotta stones pave the floor. A loft space is full of what I assume must be storage for their business. On a buffet to the left of the door is a collection of blue, green, and white ceramic olive oil containers. There are light brown baskets, and colorful containers.

"We love the old ways," Janet says. "On cold nights, we would often find ourselves in the processing plant. Those places were always busy, twenty-four hours a day, in the midst of the harvest. A nona, a grandmother, would sit near a large open fireplace that she kept an eye on throughout the long days and nights of the harvest and crush. There was always lots of food for the workers. It is now a thing of the past because so much of the process has been automated.

"And when that first lovely golden trickle of oil appears at the end of the crush and filtration process, it is worth all of the work. We love that moment, especially.

"These," she says, pointing as Stefano appears from the back room of the workshop, "are some of the gift baskets we have created over the past several years for clients. We now sell to companies and customers in Japan and, of course, all over the United States."

Stefano picks up a beautiful paper-covered box. The pattern on it looks like stone, or stucco.

"These are the boxes that we used a few years ago to ship our gifts in," he says. "The paper is actually from a photo I took of the wall of the small chapel outside our workshop. It made the box look nicer, I think." I agree.

"Come, we will show you the oils." Janet leads me into a very clean work area, just off of the main room. The floor is patterned with smooth tiles. Large, shiny stainless-steel containers line the walls. In the center of the room there is a small metal table and several small jars.

"Once the oil has been crushed, we bring it here and place it in these holding tanks," Janet explains. "Over time, the sediment settles to the bottom of the containers. We decant off the clear oil, over and over again, as the sediment continues to settle."

She slowly pours a small amount of oil, the color of gold, into a blue tasting glass.

"You have to warm the oil like this." The small glass is cupped in her hands. She gently swirls the rich, thick, golden fluid in the container.

"Smell." She holds up the jar. I close my eyes and inhale; odors of grass, pepper, and a subtle hint of wildflowers come to me.

"What kind of olive oil have I been buying all these years back in the United States?" I ask. How could something so fresh be shipped to the States and still retain such freshness?

"We can only ship a very few bottles to our clients and customers." Stefano smiles, takes the glass from Janet, and breathes in the aroma.

"So wonderful," he whispers into the room. "We are so sorry, but we haven't much time this morning to show you more. It will be a beautiful day and we have much work to do."

"I understand." The jar goes back on the table, and we walk back into the large center room of the workshop. "Thank you for sharing this with me."

"You are most welcome. Perhaps you can help with the harvest someday." Stefano is putting on his jacket as he opens the main door of the shop. "We need all the help we can get." He smiles.

Janet adds, "We have friends from the Boston area who come over every year just to help with the harvest. All of them all are of great help to us when we need it the most."

I promise to return to help when I can. They get into their small truck and quickly drive away down the hill towards the groves. I wave them good-bye.

Deep red tendrils of Virginia creeper fall down the front overhang of their studio. The ground is blanketed with crimson and fading gold leaves. Gravel crunches under my shoes as I walk into the center of what once was the borgo. A brisk cold wind blows around the corner of a small chapel across the courtyard. Leaves continue to fall from the vines above the door to their workshop. Janet and Stefano must, I imagine, look forward to the cold winter season when they can work on their beloved olive oil, pack and ship small containers of the harvest to customers and friends. They are simply two people who share deep passion for their labor and the produce of the land. They live a simple life in a small home on a hillside between Florence and Impruneta. They have not only survived, they have thrived. Their business grows, gradually, year to year, as they bring more people to the art of handmade olive oil.

Olive trees up the road shimmer in the wind. I think about the cycle of the seasons that provides this gregarious couple with their livelihood. The rains of spring arouse blossoms. Olives grow and ripen in the heat of full summer. Fall brings the harvest, when a golden aromatic liquid that has been nourished by the soils of Tuscany is placed in bottles. In the chill of winter's cold embrace it is shipped to a fortunate few.

When we taste that oil, we savor the seasons of an Italian year—a year in which the olives have gained their luscious fullness. In the hands of a dedicated couple in a stone workshop called Sagittario, those olives become more than mere oil. In the midst of our remembering where, and how, the oil came to be, we gain an even deeper understanding of the wonderful, complex, confusing, and incredible culture of Italia.

Il Torchio

Benvenuto Cellini's bust stands at the high point of the Ponte Vecchio, the old bridge that spans the river Arno in the heart of Florence. His work in gold established him as the father of that art form. Surrounding the base of his bust is a black iron fence. A local tradition says that when lovers write their names on the locks, secure them on the fence and throw the key into the river Arno, their love will never end. The fence is nearly covered with bronze and steel locks.

To the north of the Ponte Vecchio are the majority of the most famous sites in the city—the Cathedral, the Palazzo Vecchio (City Hall), and the Uffizi and Accademia museums. On this hot July afternoon, I walk south across the Ponte Vecchio, away from the crowds and museums. This is a different world; one where, in the neighborhood known as the Oltrarno, the majority of artisans have their workshops.

Via de' Bardi, one of the many streets that lead away from the south end of the bridge, is a narrow, twisting lane. A modern statue of Saint John the Baptist, patron saint of the city, stands in a small piazza where few people stop to admire the striking bronze figure.

The shadows within this small byway are a welcome retreat from the intensifying heat of this summer afternoon. On the right, about five minutes walk from Ponte Vecchio, is the tiny workshop of Il Torchio (The Press). As I enter the shop, a small bell above the door announces my arrival. A woman with bright green eyes and lightly gray-streaked hair walks up and offers her hand. I note a strong and firm grip.

"I am Anna Anichini," she informs me.

"It is a pleasure to meet you, Signora."

"May I help you with anything today?"

I look around the shop. The shelves are lined with elegant leather-covered journals and address books. Some of the covers are embossed with symbols of the city. Other covers are glass-smooth and shiny. A wooden rack displays intricately colored sheets of marbled paper, a specialty of Florentine artisans since the 1700s.

"So many beautiful things. I think I will just look around for a few moments, if I may."

She smiles. "Of course. If I can answer any questions, please let me know."

A mahogany brown leather-bound journal attracts my eye. The leather is smooth with a luminous hand rubbed finish. It makes a cracking sound as I open it. An embossed mark on the inside cover identifies the maker as Il Torchio, Firenze. The pages are rough-edged, the paper finely textured to the touch. The pages are stitched together by hand. This is a work of high quality, made with meticulous care.

There are three women, including Anna, sitting around a large work table in the back of the shop. Sheets of paper, thread, scissors, and various-sized pieces of leather in a medley of colors, are scattered and stacked on the table.

"Excuse me, Signora."

Anna looks up.

"This journal is so incredibly beautiful and detailed."

She rises from the stool on the opposite side of the table. "I am the owner of this shop. Thank you for your kind comment."

"How did you come to own this place?"

"Please." She motions to an empty seat at the work table. "This is Maria, and this is Carla." The women look up for a moment. Maria has large brown eyes and thick black hair. There is a calm demeanor about her, one that immediately sets me at ease. Carla's red hair, bright blue eyes, freckled nose, and amber-colored eyeglass frames give the impression of youth and energy. There is a confident air about her. Both women smile and return to their work.

Anna explains, "I own a home that is full of books: photo books, journals, and old leather-bound novels. Bookbinding has always fascinated me, especially the traditional methods. My goal has been to create a place where the art of bookbinding would not only survive, but thrive. In 1980 I found this space. It had been empty for a great many years, certainly at least since the floods of 1966. I wanted it the moment I walked in."

Carla picks up a long needle and thread. She begins, very slowly and precisely, to sew the pages of a journal together. Maria uses a glue-covered brush to place thick beige paper on the inside cover of a deep blue leather-bound journal.

"After I took this space," Anna continues, "I had to clean it up and, of course, had to get paper and leather to work with. Several family friends were able to help me. They knew a few dedicated craftsmen who could supply me with the raw materials I needed to get started. People who visited the shop would tell others. Soon enough, a lot of my business was referral. Now, much of our business is by mail, over the Internet, and by a few suppliers in the United States."

She looks across as Carla and Maria continue to work. "I am so very proud of our work. We use only traditional methods, from the Renaissance. Some of the crafts of book-binding date back to the Middle Ages."

"Incredible" is the only word that comes to my mind.

"My daughter, there," Anna says, nodding toward Maria, "will soon take over the business for me. It is time that I have the opportunity to rest and relax just a bit."

"So the next generation will help ensure that these traditions are not lost," I remark.

"Yes," she replies, "and as it should be. I continue to study the history of Florence and especially the art of paper and leather. If the artisans and craftsmen who preceded us in this work had not written down what they had learned, and had not cared enough to let others share in their knowledge, then my products would be poorer, indeed."

We sit for a few moments in silence as I watch Carla and Maria work. The stillness in the shop is interrupted only by the noise of a car or motorcycle out on the street. I hear the small pop as Carla's needle pierces paper, followed by the sound of the thread being pulled through to bind the sheets together. Maria has since moved on to another book in which she glues gorgeous fleur-de-lis-patterned paper. The glue brush makes a *clink* as it is placed back in the glass container.

A couple opens the door to the shop and enters.

"Well, I suppose I should be going. I would like to purchase this one journal, if I may."

"But of course." Anna stands and picks up a small pad from among the stacks of paper and leather on the work table. She writes down the amount due. I pay her, take the receipt, and prepare to leave.

"Thank you, Maria, Carla, and Signora Anichini, for your time."

Anna walks over to greet the new customers. I excuse myself as I pass them. The bell overhead rings again as I slowly close the brass-framed glass door to the shop.

Nearly an hour has passed in the course of our discussion. The sun is low in the sky. Swallows flash by overhead in the thin patch of light between buildings above the narrow street. The art of creating journals and paper is not simply art, but a necessity. Births and deaths, memories of ancestors, necessities of commerce were all inked onto pages of books much like those produced at Il Torchio. I stand for a moment outside the shop and try to imagine how many workshops of artisans have come and gone through the centuries along Via de' Bardi.

When Renaissance scribes created their manuscripts and printers made hand-printed books, they used paper created by artisans not unlike Anna, women and men who carry a deep passion for their craft. The culture of Italy unfolds in a special way when we open a leather-bound journal and write on pages that have been so lovingly sewn together. Quality, time, and care all meet when an object of such beauty comes into our lives. How fortunate we are that such passion can still be found in these workshops.

On the Ponte Vecchio, the bust of Cellini stands surrounded by the locks of lovers whose hopes are sustained by the act of throwing a key into the river Arno. Along narrow lanes that cross the Oltrarno are workshops of artisans whose passion for what hands can create inspires us all.

The Workshop of Saverio Pastor

Sweet odors of wood, freshly chipped from blocks of oak, black walnut, and maple, surround a large vise on the floor of a shop. Stacks of wood line the right hand wall of the "laboratorio." On the left wall are numerous oars, from large curved scepters to small, simple boating styles. Each one lies on shelves awaiting its turn at the hand of the master in this rare and special place near the church of Madonna della Salute in Venice.

Saverio Pastor is a quiet man. He wears a green cap that covers his graying hair. Pale blue eyes greet from behind wire-rimmed glasses. He has a distracted, detached quality about him, as if the intrusion of visitors disturbs his thoughts and the mood of the wood. His manner, however, belies a much deeper affection for the art he creates: the necessary components of a gondola. The gondolas that traverse the canals of this floating city *are* Venice—and Saverio Pastor remains very busy.

A large carved piece of wood is clamped tightly between the sides of a padded vise. The sensuously curved piece is about four feet long, with a shapely curved neck that twists at one end. There is an arch, smoothed to a near-glass finish, in which a gondolier will one day rotate and twist his oar as he navigates the canals of the city. At the base is a simple straight cut of wood. It looks like a perfectly cut piece of a puzzle, something that might well fit on a gondola.

This is the forcola, the wooden piece upon which the oar rests as the gondolier steers his vessel into and around the city's narrow, twisting canals. It is, in the study of the gondola, the heart of the boat. It will serve as the fulcrum of the oar, balancing it as the gondolier propels and steers the boat. Well carved, appropriately cared for, these pieces may last as long as thirty years. Over the course of centuries, the craft of creating the forcola, once nearly extinct, has been refined to a high art.

Several years ago, Saverio was instrumental in creating an association for the preservation of the gondola, El Fèlze. Where there were once numerous gondola workshops across Venice, only a few remain today. Master craftsmen and their apprentices work through each day, learning and refining the specialized creation of the most identifiable symbol of the city.

We speak of his passion for this art.

"Wood lasts," Saverio says, smiling. "I learned from a master craftsman, Giuseppe Carli, you must allow wood to age in the forest. It becomes stronger with age. Out in the Veneto nearby, I find trees, sometimes over a hundred years old, that are at long last willing to give up their life for the gondola. I treasure this wood."

He places his hand on the piece he is working on and lovingly caresses the smooth curve where the oar will rest. It is the touch of a man consumed by something beyond words for the work he so loves. Soft, calming music floats through the dusty air, sweetened by the scent of the cured wood and his steady presence.

"I think," he begins to say as he walks across the workshop, "sometimes of the gondolas across the city." He stares out the front window of his shop to the canal. "My work supports the oars of Venice; every day one of my creations helps preserve the beauty, the incredible beauty, of the gondola." He pauses. "It is a strange boat, you know?"

"Ah, yes?" I reply.

He takes me over to a small table. There is a model of a gondola exposed to its frame.

"Look," he says. "The boat bends, the keel turns away from the bow, all done to support the balance of the gondoliers."

I study the piece. Sculpture. A piece of precious art to its bones. "It is truly beautiful."

The music has stopped. I can hear water as it laps against the walls of the canal. The workshop is silent. He begins to return to his work.

"Mille grazie," I say as I prepare to leave. *A thousand thanks.*

"It's nothing. Thank you for caring." Safety glasses are pulled down over his wire-rims, and he bends once again to his craft.

Across Venice, thanks to craftsmen like Saverio Pastor, gondolas still exist to carry the dreams of the world. Memories are created as visitors recline and watch gondoliers guide their boats past palazzos, museums, and churches of the city. Deep inside those boats, fingers of wood softly support panels and metals, burnished by years of tender care.

I step out into the late afternoon light. A gondola floats by. The gondolier swings the boat with his oar, the forcola responds. They move as one.

Street Music

Music echoes in the streets of Italy. At any given moment, around any corner, you may be greeted by the music of a string quartet. You may walk into a piazza and find a guitarist playing music of the ancient—and current—masters. The haunting sounds of an opera aria may greet you as you stroll back to your canalside hotel in Venice. Harpsichord music may surprise you in an ancient fort perched high above a hill town in Tuscany.

These musicians enrich Italian life. Cities and towns often seem more complete with informal but passionate music. People take time to stop and listen; the notes remind visitors of this country's rich and varied musical heritage, and enhance the moments we share amid places of beauty and history.

VENICE

The Accademia Bridge is a Venetian treasure. It spans the width of the Grand Canal, connecting the area of Dorsoduro, and its world famous museum, with the area of San Marco. Several years ago, the city rose up to save the bridge from sure destruction. Funds were raised, and the bridge was rescued. The restoration is gorgeous.

Night has fallen on the city, and crowds have dwindled. There are a few people on the bridge as I stand and look down at the long stretch of palazzos that line both sides of the Grand Canal. As I walk down the long, sloping steps of the bridge, and stroll along a narrow lane, I come to a small piazza outside of a church. Huge, dark oak doors are open to the evening, and notes of music float around me. The familiar composition is that of Vivaldi, a favorite Venetian son. *The Four Seasons* is being played by a group of musicians inside the church. I walk up the few steps to the doors.

I enter the church and stand against the back wall; all of the seats are taken. The nave of the church is dark. I can barely make out the audience in the shadows. Candles flicker atop the altar, and spotlights shine on a group of musicians gently drawing their bows across the strings of viola, violin, and cello. A young woman sits at the keyboard of a harpsichord. The rich, deep, luminous finish of her instrument reflects the candlelight as she bends over the keys to her music.

The smell of earth mixes with the scents of burning candles and fills the church. I close my eyes and time seems to stop. Thoughts of all of the people who came here over the centuries, for Mass, for concerts, for quiet retreat, or for heartfelt confession come to me. The music continues. I leave the church at the conclusion of one section of Vivaldi's famous concerto.

Outside, an older couple, nearly invisible in the darkness, are seated on a bench. They listen to the music, eyes closed, as I quietly walk by. They hold hands and seem lost in the music and the moment. The music follows and surrounds me as I slowly make my way farther along a narrow passageway. A young woman sits on the sill of an open upstairs window. Her head leans back against the frame of the window as she listens to the music. If she hears my approach on the walkway, she doesn't move.

When I arrive in the Campo San Sebastian the music is a faint breath in the still night air. Venice and the music of Italians provide once again a moment of reflection, wonderment, and gratitude.

FLORENCE

Piazza della Repubblica, in the center of Florence, was built in the late 1800s. Many famous and historic buildings, including the Jewish ghetto, were torn down in preparation for the city's role (albeit short-lived) as the capital of Italy. The only reminder of the market that once occupied some of this area is a large column, topped by a statue of "Abundance." The Piazza is now the largest public space in the heart of the old city. In the course of any day thousands of visitors walk across the piazza; some rest their weary feet on benches placed along the perimeter of the square. On this warm afternoon, in the shadow of the column, a crowd has gathered to listen to a musician.

A young man is bowed low over the sensuous curves of his guitar. His dark hair flutters in the breeze as he concentrates and gently plays the instrument. His left leg is raised on a small footstool. Other than the movement of his hand, his body is alert and focused. The sound of music that rises from the guitar draws more and more people who want to hear this splendid musician play. At the start of a break, I approach him and ask how he came to play in Florence.

Tadeusz Machalski came to Italy several years ago by way of Seville, Spain, where he studied classical guitar. He was born and raised in Poland. In the course of his life he has also lived in England and, for a short time, in the United States. Tadeusz's shy smile shows his pride at sharing such an art with those who care to listen. He has dark, deep-set eyes and coal-black hair. His slight frame supports an athletic body that is most notable for large, muscular hands that remind me of those of Michelangelo's David. I thank him for his time as he returns to his performance.

The crowd listens intently to many beautifully played pieces. Sounds of a master fill the center of the large square and, on occasion, the music echoes from nearby buildings. Enthusiastic applause greets the completion of every piece. I linger to enjoy his art for a few moments longer, then move on, grateful for such melodious street music.

Several weeks later, as I stroll near Piazza San Marco in Venice, I again hear guitar music. A small crowd has gathered around someone playing the instrument on a particularly cool fall evening. The music is indeed being played by Tadeusz. He interprets a selection of Renaissance and classical pieces. He smiles as he looks up at the conclusion of one piece. The audience replies with appreciative applause.

Light from a full moon casts gray-patterned shadows on the stones of the small piazza where he plays. A boat's horn echoes into the night air. The persistent rumble of a water taxi's engine vibrates nearby. Sounds of dinner—hushed conversation, the clink of glassware and the metallic scrape of utensils—float out of a canalside café. The music adds to the experience of this most mysterious of Italian cities. When we all are given the time to simply stand or sit and listen, the city becomes even more timeless. Couples lean against each other as more people gather to listen.

The music continues to trace my steps as I turn corners in dark, narrow alleyways. Harsher urban sounds overpower notes no longer loud enough to be heard in the heart of the city. I believe, however, that I can still hear their faint and haunting tones as I slowly drift off to sleep.

SAN GIMIGNANO

The Rocca, or fortress, of the walled hill town of San Gimignano occupies the highest ground in the city. It provides unobstructed views over the hills of southern Tuscany. From the piazza of the Duomo (cathedral) of the city, I walk up a steep and sinuous roadway. Heat from an October noonday sun beats down on the nearly empty streets of the town. I turn at the top of the road and walk past the ancient arched gate of the fortress. Several olive trees fill the center of this medieval ruin. A few cats prowl through the underbrush. Leaves are scattered at my feet.

Suddenly, the precise notes of harpsichord and harp music fill the space. A pair of musicians are seated under an archway in the corner of the fort. He bends and weaves over the keyboard as she, eyes closed, gently strokes the strings of a golden brown harp. I walk over and stand to listen as they continue to play. During a break in the music, I ask them how they came to play at such a beautiful location. Giovanni, as he introduces himself, is a young man from Milan. He has deep green eyes, shoulder-length black hair, and a strong, confident face. He introduces me to Caterina. She is a blonde-haired stunner; blue eyes, a fine jawline, and high cheek bones give her face softness, approachability, and an ease that somehow matches the beauty of the music and her instrument.

"We met seven years ago on the streets of this town," he says. "I was to study music with a harpsichord master who lived here. Little did I know that Caterina was here to study music as well."

The wind pushes some sheets of music off her stand. As she bends down to pick them up she adds, "It was as if we both had known each other from the very beginning of our lives. I was born and raised in Verona and had never before been to San Gimignano."

The sheet music is placed back on the stand. He reaches over and takes her hand.

"We are here," he continues, "because we love Italy, this town, and music. Whatever pleasure we provide to visitors is our joy. We find that playing up here brings life back to the walls. It is only when we have shared the music that was written when these walls were being built that we feel connected to the people who lived here in the past."

"And," Caterina adds, "it is always a delight to share that connection with those who come here. When we first met, the town was less popular than it is today. We are amazed at the number of visitors who share a passion for our country's history."

They return to their instruments. Once again, the space is filled with the notes of the ancient music. Caterina, Giovanni and I can feel the presence of those who built these walls; we can more deeply appreciate how music connects all generations in a way that is beyond explanation.

ARIA IN VENICE

Late on a warm summer's evening, I am returning to my hotel in Venice. There is no breeze, and I pause beside a wall to take in the silence of the city. As I stand, arms leaned against ancient brick, the sounds of a soprano singing an aria float between the buildings. As silently as a breath, the silver crenellated bow of an ebony gondola appears from beneath one of the bridges. A lit candle, suspended in a glass holder, swings gently over the forward section of the boat. As the music continues, the gondola moves into full view. Two lovers recline on rich brocaded cushions. Their eyes are closed. The gondolier leans and guides his craft deftly down the darkened, narrow, canal. A final quiet swirl of the oar, and the gondola disappears around the corner of a nearby palazzo. The music fades away.

Italian street music enriches our experiences in this country. Notes that greet our ears around corners of narrow streets, the gentle voice of a soprano on a still summer's night, and the quartets that play in squares across Italy bring the culture to us. Whether we have experienced it in a city piazza, along the coast, or in a church, most assuredly the memory is enriched by the sounds of music.

Carver of Dreams

When Rosanno Rondoni was a young boy, his brother Roberto says, he wanted to hold every carving tool and piece of wood he could find. Roberto and his wife, Venanzia, have invited me into their home in Assisi for dinner. In the course of our conversation, Roberto mentions his brother's workshop.

"He has read and studied woodworking, sculpture, and anything that had to do with the creation of three dimensional arts for most of his life.

"Throughout the first thirty-five years of his life," Roberto continues, "Rosanno worked in what you might call 'normal work.' He worked with me as an electrician, always chasing the best way to make an income. Yet there was always something gnawing inside him, something that he wanted to explore. It was in 1995, during a conversation with him, that I encouraged him to pursue his passion. From that moment on, Rosanno wanted nothing more than to work with his hands as a wood sculptor. He wanted to create great beauty for clients from the visions of his artistic dreams."

It is an unusually cool early June morning when I enter Rosanno's workshop. He shakes my hand; his grip is strong and confident. His features are classic Italian: dark brown eyes and thick black eyebrows are framed in an open and inviting face. A well-trimmed goatee, broad smile, and strong jawline define a face of passion and strong character.

Music fills Rosanno's workshop and spills into the narrow street known as the Via Fontabella in Assisi. It is music from the soundtrack of the motion picture *The Horse Whisperer*. When Thomas Newman wrote the music for the film, I rather imagine that he could little have imagined his music would inspire a woodcarver in Assisi. Yet, so it is. The music fired in the imagination of a man thousands of miles away—about another man who communicates with horses in the most spiritual of ways—fills the small workshop where Rosanno works.

He excuses himself to turn down the music. I encourage him to leave it loud, to let it inspire his imagination and encourage his work. In the course of our conversation, we share a common bond of interest in Newman's music: we both find it inspirational for the creation of what our passions motivate within us. Rosanno has a rare talent. He shares with me that he has never been formally trained in woodcarving, yet the piece upon which he works, a frieze of putti (angels) and scrolls, is as complex and beautiful a piece as I have ever seen.

Stacks of workbooks—copies—of the writings and sketches of Michelangelo and Leonardo da Vinci lie open on a chair. On those pages, angels vie with horses for his attention and his unerring eye.

"I am always reading and studying the masters. They have much to teach, even now. I can never learn enough." He slowly turns a page.

The room smells of fresh-cut wood and the heavy scent of sap. I ask him to please continue his work so that I can photograph him in the course of his labors. He eagerly begins to walk towards his workbench.

"You know," he says in Italian, "I always had hoped that I could make this dream of mine come true. And now it has. Certainly money is part of the reason I do this work, but first and always foremost is the art and my passion for it. Without that, I may as well go back to wiring electricity in people's houses." He shakes his head.

"Not that such work is not good! Roberto, my brother, does it very well. It's just that. . . ." His voice tapers off. He picks up a chisel from the neat array of tools behind him and begins to work on the piece on the workbench. His large hands confidently move in a ballet of twists and turns that are accentuated by the rapping of his mallet on the chisel. Chips of walnut fly across the workbench. I watch for several minutes before he puts the tool back down and faces me.

"It's just that I don't think life is long enough, now, for me to go back to that work. I would do almost anything to continue"—he opens his right hand and sweeps through a corner of the workshop—"all and any of this."

He strolls over to a large format book that lies open to a page of writings of Michelangelo. "He was a great man," Rosanno says, as he gently strokes the pages of the book. "Did you know that he wrote poetry?" I share with him that I've read some of Michelangelo's poems. He smiles, clearly satisfied that ancient words still inspire work as varied as carving and writing.

After thanking Rosanno, I walk down the steep street that fronts his workshop. I find a place where there is an unobstructed view out over the valley below Assisi. The music of the workshop quietly echoes across the street. I take in a view that has seen much change since the days of Saint Francis and Saint Clare.

Yet, somewhere in the centuries that have passed, great passions—deep and intense fires—survive. They fuel the creative genius in the heart and soul of a one-time electrician who now brings life to wood. By living and working with that passion, he inspires others. He knows what he must do always comes first and, by so putting his art first, he inspires others to follow their dreams. In workshops throughout Italy, throughout our world, such passions give life to the arts and the sciences. So it was in the Renaissance; so it is today.

Hounds of the Lord

 seemingly innocent, rather nonde-script friar from the northern Italian city of Ferrara arrived in Florence in the spring of 1492. Few who saw the diminutive monk with dark brooding eyes and large hawklike nose could have envisioned that his residency at the Monastery of San Marco would profoundly alter the history of Florence and the entire art world. A Dominican monk, Girolamo Savonarola was impassioned with a verve and energy that soon took all of Florence under its spell. His sermons, preached at the Cathedral of Santa Maria del Fiore, increasingly gave vent to his visions of impending doom and suffering for Florentines if they did not immediately mend their sinful ways.

Florentines maintain to this day a reputation for being particularly liberal when it comes to matters of the flesh. They have always enjoyed an easy style and pace of life. Their interpretations of biblical teachings were far more permissive than anything one simple monk might have to say. However, more and more of the citizens attended, or were recruited, to hear this friar speak. Come they did. By the early part of 1494, the entire cathedral was packed on Sundays with anxious—some say almost hypnotized—listeners who began to believe the prophecies of Savonarola.

The leaders of the Inquisition in the Roman Catholic Church at the time were hand-picked specifically from the Dominican order. Their Latin name, "Canes Sacrae," seems particularly appropriate: "Hounds of the Lord." Inquisitors pursued with a vengeance those charged with violating church law. The history of the Inquisition stands as strong testament to their skills and talents.

The Medici family of Florence, long in power, had begun to lose its support within the city. By the summer of 1494 they had been expelled to their country homes, victims of the wary and politically astute Signoria—the governing council of the city. The Medici had been particularly singled out by Savonarola for their blatant display of wealth. In the shadow of their departure all "vanities," as the fanatical monk called them, were to be destroyed. On one afternoon and evening in the fall of 1494, paintings by Botticelli and Raphael, the books of Dante and the Greek philosophers, and countless family treasures were turned to ash on the "Bonfire of the Vanities." The monk began to present himself as a prophet, something that Pope Alexander VI down in Rome did not take favorably. Only one member of the church could directly hear the word of God—and that was the Pope.

Alexander threatened excommunication of the Dominican if he persisted. But Savonarola did not relent. Florentines tired of his prophetic ravings. The population began to miss the more liberal days of greater freedom. The Medici were kept informed and in due time they returned to their positions of power in the city. In May 1498 Savonarola was arrested and hanged, his body burned in the large square that fronts the city hall. A memorial marker near the fountain of Neptune in the Piazza della Signoria marks the spot where he was burned. The Florentines wanted the monk to go away; they also did not want to forget the lessons he taught the city.

When the ashes of Savonarola's body were gathered together after his execution, members of the clergy collected them, took them the ancient bridge in the center of the city—the Ponte Vecchio—and scattered his ashes in the Arno River. At the time of his death, the bridge was still used as a butcher shop of Florence. The local story says that as the butchers tossed the offal into the river, the residents of Pisa, downriver, were getting only what they deserved—the worst parts of slaughtered animals. To this day, no love is lost between the two cities. So it goes.

Inside the Monastery of San Marco, individual cells are frescoed with various scenes from the life of the Christ. Visitors can stand at the door of Savonarola's cell and imagine the words spoken, the prayers given, in the course of his mission. In the centuries that have passed, more and more people have come to understand the incalculable worth of the items destroyed in the bonfire. The ashes that were whipped into the sky over Florence that dark day carried the remains of some great pieces of art. I am certain that the judges who found him guilty kept that in mind when the monk was sentenced to punishment by hanging and burning.

On a recent afternoon, a young man took a can of black spray paint and defaced the memorial to Savonarola in the city square. Local authorities had known of this young man's instability and arrested him shortly after the crime. Within an hour, the paint was gone, the memorial restored to its original condition. People gathered to see the vandalized marker. Where once flames reached into the air above the crowds, now the curious visitors looked *down* to see the monk's place of remembrance. The ashes of his fires are long since spent, washed away by the rains of centuries. For all the fear that the Dominican "hounds" brought to the populations of Italy and the rest of Europe, their time is long past. Yet the shadow of the man and his fanatical ravings remains present in the city. What might we have if the books and canvases by those great artists had not been destroyed? What treasures might we all still have to appreciate? There is some justice.

I imagine that deep in the mud of the Arno, along its wide and sinuous path, the remains of a certain monk share space with the detritus of the centuries. Fanaticism reclaimed by nature, a gift from the divine power; Hounds of the Lord, indeed.

In Search of Lorenzo

Handwritten documents captured the history of Italy. The Archivio di Stato di Firenze (Archives of the city) occupies a large building at Viale Giovine Italia, 6, in Florence. The Viale is a major roadway that encircles the city. Built in the nineteenth century over the foundations of the city's walls, it is a constant whir of activity. Cars, buses, mopeds, all vie for space every hour of the day. But stored within the archive, and accessible to scholars and those interested in research, are letters, contracts, and other hand-written documents dating to the late Middle Ages.

I have come to the archive in search of Lorenzo di Medici. The Medici family was the most powerful financial and political force in Renaissance Tuscany. Giovanni di

Bicci, the patriarch of the family, founded a bank in the mid-fourteenth century. Lorenzo was one of two sons, born to Piero de Medici (known as Il Gottoso—The Gouty—due to his poor health) and his wife, Lucrezia Tornabuoni. By the time leadership of the family passed to him, there were eleven branches of the bank throughout Europe. The Medici had become wealthy beyond imagining.

In 1469, Lorenzo assumed leadership over both the banking empire and the city council of Florence. He lived through an assassination attempt that took his younger brother's life in 1478. An artist as well as a politician, he wrote poetry and music, encouraged the arts, and inspired generations after him to continue the family's artistic patronage. The documentation required to keep the far-flung banking empire in operation was enormous. The family's responsibilities involved complicated legal negotiations as well as replies to inquiries of all kinds. Many of those ancient documents are kept in the vaults of the archive. We know Lorenzo by his portrait, and by the poetry he left behind; but what of the man's handwriting? What could it tell us about his creative drive, his leadership, and his passions?

My bags are searched and screened before I am allowed to enter the archive. Admission requires the completion of several forms and review of my passport. Plastic admission card in hand, I walk into the research room to begin my quest. Long oak tables are neatly aligned on both sides of a large, well-lighted room. Students, scholars, researchers lean over documents and books. Some use laptop computers to record notes of their discoveries. Others simply write on paper tablets.

An employee of the archive says that numerous documents are available that were written by, or signed by, Lorenzo. I am directed to a small room where she says I should wait. Several minutes later she arrives with a large blue leather portfolio. She lays the luminous polished case on the table in front of me. I am given a large magnifying glass as well as a pair of white cotton gloves. As she unties the portfolio and opens it, I put on the gloves.

Spread before me is a stack of documents from the years 1496 to 1499. They are presented with a sheet of fine paper separating each ancient correspondence. The archivist explains that I have two hours in which to review the contents. At the conclusion of that time, I must return the portfolio to her. She points out a camera in the room, further evidence of the serious steps taken to protect these invaluable records of Italian history.

Lorenzo wrote with a measured script. The spacing between letters is neat, carefully figured, and precisely inked on the page. The distance between lines is even. His signature, however, is written large and in a graceful fashion. His first name is all that appears in his signature on all the documents. People knew of him and required no further clarification as to "which Lorenzo" he was. The signature is strong. Bold, thick lines underscore each sweep of the pen on every letter. Lorenzo was, it appears from his writing, bold and decisive. As I lean over the signature with the magnifying glass it occurs to me that I am seeing a man's signature, part of his legacy, from more than five hundred years ago. We enjoy the Florence of today because this man was driven to lead, and because he loved the arts.

There are letters requesting that an artist complete a commission. Contracts sent to a bank in Antwerp mention interest on loans. A letter written to the leaders of Florence's governing council records notes of a past meeting. At the end of only an hour, I have seen enough. The magnitude of history that I have seen will take time to settle. It is one thing to view the correspondence, another altogether to make some further sense of it all.

Several days later, I walk to the Piazza della Signoria, the large square in front of the city hall of Florence. After being seated, I take out my journal and begin to write the story of the archive. A woman arrives at the café. She takes a seat at a nearby table. Her cell phone appears and she begins to feverishly type a text message. As I take pen to paper it occurs to me that, while technology has enabled so much of our day-to-day living, perhaps writing by hand to record our thoughts and dreams, our commitments and our cares, isn't such an antiquated idea.

Had it not been for those who learned to write, who understood the importance of keeping documents and who cared about art, the city of Florence—all of Europe for that matter—would be different indeed. When we sit to write a postcard home, or a letter, we pay homage to men like Lorenzo di Medici. Did I find Lorenzo? Not really. What I did find, however, was a connection to the past, historical records that unite the stones and streets, the museums and churches. Lorenzo's legacy *is* Florence, recorded in every sweeping arc of the signature he left behind.

When I leave the café, I stroll over to the Uffizi Gallery. In the halls above me are over forty-five galleries full of art that the Medici family brought to Florence. History is written, many say, by the winners of wars. I think it enough to remember ancient papers, locked in a vault across the city. We are, after all is said and done, connected to generations past. How grateful I am to know that what *we* write might just survive.

Epilogue

Remains

**P**olitical and cultural lines that once clearly delineated where the culture of one country started and the other ended are slowly disappearing. Technology and ease of travel bring people to places that they never could have visited even a generation ago.

The shuttle driver who brings me to my hotel near Milan is from Pakistan. Despite earthquakes and political instability he expresses longing for his homeland, even after fourteen years in Italy. Workers who harvest olives on an estate near Florence (owned by an Italian man and his Norwegian wife) are from the old Bulgaria. They talk to their capo—boss—among the olives in a type of sign language-cum-confusion. Receptionists at hotels are Japanese, Chinese, Indian, and Senegalese. They all speak an Italian that crosses borders, slurs the language, and erodes

131

the clarity of a musical idiom that had once been pure and classical. In cities across this splendid country thousands of tourists from Moscow's nouveau riche blend with Brazilians, Australians, and Indonesians in a kind of group dance. They swirl across piazzas, one language replacing another as they "experience Italy."

Visitors across Europe dress increasingly alike. Once blue jeans were considered the anathema of Italian tastes. Now bare navels appear on hip-hugged Italians who wear them as high style. Walking shoes are everywhere. White striped, world-marketed, and third-world-country-produced, such footwear is universally worn by visitors who are bearers of the "new" world culture.

Can the traditions of Bella Italia survive? I believe they can, and they will.

In spite of new generations who use cell phones like paper towels, where photographs slip through the atmosphere at amazing speed, and the great leaders of once-mighty political entities move into an uncertain future, the techno-gap simply compresses the world around us. Arriving travelers in Venice's Santa Lucia Station are greeted by a group of musicians from Peru who play Greek pan flutes while dressed as "American Indians," headdress included.

When I travel, the unique is what pulls me, entices me to a different culture. I rarely watch television when on foreign soil. I find that the world but rarely changes in the course of a year; people, politics, and weather being what they are. The cell phone is a marvel of our age and I do use it because it is the only way that family can find me while I globe-trot.

Maybe we travelers were better off when we all *didn't* want to be like everyone else in the Western world. Italy's unique culture hides just under the cover of sameness that permeates some of the nation's towns and cities: fast-food eateries, globally branded retailers, and the same music that we hear in our home countries. The menu in a small-town trattoria I recently visited offered the best of Italian food; the recorded music touched on everything from Indian chant to Nat King Cole to Edith Piaf.

What has tourism done to Italia? Billions of euros flowing into the local economy are having a positive effect on employment in cities as well as some rural areas. Yet what money often brings, and what is often desired, are the very things that mask the local culture. When travelers come to Italy, they should expect to be in Italy, and traditional Italy is getting a bit harder to find. It has always been easy in our America-centric world to judge other countries—Italy included. In spite of that, I try to remember that the first cars and motorized bicycles (okay, motorcycles) in the world were produced in Italy. The world mimics Italian design. When you say to anyone that you are going to Italy, Tuscany in particular these days, a look comes across their face that borders on blissful envy.

Travel beckons us away from what we know to what we hope to find. When we return from Rome or Florence, Venice or the Amalfi coast, what we recall is not, cannot be, a solid stream of memories. The odor of espresso may remind us of a café in Lucca; a song may take us back to a small candlelit table where we enjoyed conversation along the Amalfi coast; the russet sky of sunset may stir the memory of a beach on the Italian coast where we walked after dinner. In the open fields and small villages across the country, most Italians carry on as if nothing were changing—and that is where the true culture thrives. It is the simple day-to-day process of living that most of us remember.

Walking our way through the crowds in central Rome or Florence or Venice isn't really Italy. Rather, it is the small, uncomplicated discoveries that touch us. Those special moments are what bring us back for another visit and that won't go away once we are home.

An acquaintance shared with me that everything she loved about the Italian culture was summed up in one single moment. On a summer's afternoon she leaned out of the upstairs window of her small villa near Siena. As she looked down a cypress-lined path she watched an elderly woman, small child in hand, walk slowly up to an old bench. The woman sat, opened the bag she carried with her, and began to knit in the shadow of the trees. The young child played quietly nearby. A breeze would occasionally stir up dust along the path. This woman simply knitted, needles clicking lightly as evening approached. The culture *is* here and will be for centuries to come. Along the smaller byways of the country, away from the everyday crush of cities and technology, Italians carry on with traditions whose roots trace back well over two thousand years.

Our understanding of a culture and the memories of travel become, nearly as soon as we return home, bits and pieces of our time away—a peaceful garden, someone we met, perhaps someone we watched as they made their way, or simply the time we shared under the shelter of Italian skies.

Glossary

A dopo Colloquial expression, typically familiar, that translates as "see you later."

badia abbey

borgo When referring to the countryside in Italy it means "village." More specifically, the term is usually applied to a small number of dwellings located in very close proximity to each other. A borgo might consist of two large villas, workers' quarters, and perhaps one or two chapels used by one to three landowning families and their staffs.

campanile bell tower

doge The elected political leader of the city council in Venice. The doges led the city from 700 to 1797. Their offices were in the Palazzo Ducale (the Duke's Palace) in the Piazza San Marco.

forcola The sculpted piece of wood (usually mahogany or walnut) attached to the gondola, that is used to hold the oar in place.

loggia A covered area typically attached to a palace or other large building, constructed using a series of arches to support the roof.

nona Colloquial, familiar, for "grandmother."

Oltrarno The south side of the Arno River within the political limits of the city of Florence. Visitors usually access this part of the city by way of the Ponte Vecchio, the old bridge in the center of town.

palazzo palace

putti figures of cherubs, used in painting and sculpture

About the Author

MARK GORDON SMITH was raised in a military family and lived in Italy during the early years of his life, an experience that fueled his later love for travel. He served in the armed forces for several years after graduating from the United States Military Academy at West Point. In 2001, Mark moved to Florence to seek the fulfillment of a long goal—to practice his craft of writing. His first book, *Tuscan Echoes: A Season in Italy* was the product of that sojourn in Italy. *Tuscan Light: Memories of Italy* is the second in an anticipated trilogy.

Mark has traveled extensively throughout Europe, and for the past thirty years has focused his attention on Italy. In response to numerous requests from readers, he now leads small group tours in Italy, introducing to others many of the places he has described in his books. Through his travel firm, Private Italy (www.private-italy.com), he offers these tours in the spring and fall of each year.

Mark divides his writing time between the coast of North Carolina, the town of Creede, Colorado, and his beloved Italy.

FORTHCOMING IN 2008

The Shelter of Italian Skies

UNDERSTANDING THE CULTURE OF A COUNTRY IS A LONG and rewarding journey. In the final book of his Italian trilogy, Mark shares insights into the profound connections that all Italians have with their homeland. From the northern reaches of Lake Maggiore and Lake Como, to the southern coast of Sicily, the author brings to life the extraordinary, often hidden amidst the ordinary, moments of Italian life.

In the tradition of *Tuscan Echoes* and *Tuscan Light*, *The Shelter of Italian Skies* represents the culmination of the author's decade-long, revealing study of the Italian culture—and his lifelong love affair with the country and its people.